REBETIKA

SONGS FROM THE OLD GREEK UNDERWORLD

Edited by Katharine Butterworth
& Sara Schneider

AIORA

Katharine Butterworth is the founder and director for 25 years of "Study in Greece", an accredited college study program for juniors and seniors in Athens, based on contemporary Greek life, and as such the first of its kind. Katharine now lives in California.

Sara Schneider studied English Language and Literature at Trinity University in San Antonio, Texas. She came to Greece on holiday in 1972 and stayed.

Illustrations by Khronis Botsoglou

First edition Komboloi Press, New York, 1975
Second edition Aiora Press, Athens 2014

© Komboloi Press 1975
© Aiora Press 2014

ISBN: 978-618-5048-20-4

AIORA PRESS
11 Mavromichali st.
Athens 10679 - Greece
tel: +30 210 3839000
www.aiora.gr

Contents

Preface to the second edition

The first edition of *Rebetika* was published shortly after the fall of the military junta (1967-74). Censorship, existent at the time (it was only abolished under the new Constitution of 1975), had obscured many details of the long history of *rebetic* songs, and research on the topic was for the most part taboo. Nonetheless, Katharine Butterworth and Sara Schneider, editors of this first ever comprehensive English-language compilation of *rebetika,* succeeded in offering foreigners an insider's view into the universe of the songs of the old Greek underworld. The book delivered, and became a modern classic.

Several years have passed and times have changed. The importance of *rebetika* has been recognized, at least in Greece, and considerable research has been conducted, but the validity of the abundant information contained in the work remains impressively unaltered. Aside from the lyrics of more than fifty songs, with Greek and English parallel texts, it includes informative essays by prominent experts in the field highlighting specific aspects of the *rebetika*, as well as a glossary of Greek words with no exact equivalent in British or American culture.

This second revised and updated edition of *Rebetika* aims to help a new generation of foreign readers of the 21st century orient themselves in the intriguing "world of hash dens, brothels and songs wherein historical figures like Socrates and Xerxes occasionally make bizarre appearances among the trams and hookahs, and death is still called Charos, a corruption of Charon in ancient mythology."

Aris Laskaratos
Publisher
Athens, May 2014

Foreword

The songs in this book are a sampling of the urban folk songs of Greece during the first half of the 20th century. They are the creative expression of an urban subculture whose members the Greeks commonly called *rebetes*. These *rebetes* were people living a marginal and often underworld existence on the fringes of established society, disoriented and struggling to maintain themselves in the developing industrial ports, despised and persecuted by the rest of society. And it is the hardships and suffering of these people, their fruitless dreams, their current loves and their lost loves that these songs are about, and underlying them all, their jaunty, tough will to survive.

The appeal of these songs is that the conflicts they express are not exclusively Greek conflicts, they are everybody's; and they are still unresolved — in urban Greece as in urban America or urban Anywhere. Many young people from all over the world who come to Greece learn these songs and sing them, and in singing them recognize echoes of their own malaise and the problems that trouble us all. Our purpose in putting this book together is to carve a small opening in the barrier compounded of music, language, and culture that has limited *rebetic* songs chiefly to Greece. This volume in no way claims to be the final word on the subject; it is but a beginning. And if it succeeds in generating interest in *rebetika* we will have achieved our aim.

The book is for anyone interested in modern Greece, but it was the interest of students whom we have known in Greece that engendered the idea of this book, and therefore we have provided the songs also in Greek. Ideally recorded music and filmed dances should accompany the book, because it is essential to try to grasp the original style and spirit of these songs. However, there do exist authentic recordings of the old *rebetic* singers such as Sotiria Bellou, Markos Vamvakaris, Marika Ninou, Mitsakis, Stratos, Mouflouzelis, etc., and time should be spent listening to these recordings, feeling the rhythms, absorbing the style. The printed musical examples in this book will then be within easy reach.

Because the *rebetika* were originally created and performed as a fusion of music, lyrics, and dance, we have attempted to examine them in this light, and we owe an unrepayable debt of gratitude to Markos Dragoumis is for his essay on the music, to Ted Petrides for his essay on the dances, and to Elias Petropoulos, who not only wrote the general introduction but also permitted us to use the song texts from his anthology *REBETIKA TRAGOUDIA*, and gave us invaluable help with the argot of the Greek underworld. We are equally grateful to Sakis Papadimitriou for his comparison of blues with *rebetika*, and to Khronis Botsoglou for his illustrations. All these men contributed to this book without promise or hope of reward. Warmest thanks are also due to countless Greek and American friends for their counsel and support, but we especially thank Electra Petropoulos and Iannis Masouras for their painstaking conceptual explanations in the early stages of the translations, Athan Anagnostopoulos, who encouraged us to go ahead when we were getting cold feet, and David Hardy, who in the final stages of preparation cast a hard and critical Sheffield eye over the entire work.

Katharine Butterworth
Sara Schneider
Athens, April 1975

Rebetika

Around 1920 the poor people of urban Greece began singing songs of a special type, filled with complaint and desire, love and bitterness; they were melancholy songs telling of the misfortunes of these obscure people. These songs are known as *rebetika*. Their popularity increased during the period of the Greek Civil War (1946-49), and after 1950 all the Greeks were singing them. This latter period of general popularity, however, was accompanied by a rapid decline in the quality of the songs themselves, and today they are no longer being composed.

The origins of the *rebetika* are much older. The songs first appeared in the mid 1800's and were the songs of the Greek underworld. Until 1920 the *rebetika* were sung exclusively within the underworld. This urban subculture was a segment of the lowest socioeconomic class in Greece, and its members were known as *rebetes* or *manges*. Though it is difficult to define a *rebetis* or a *mangas*, it can be said that he was a person who lived outside the accepted standards of the traditional Greek society, and who showed contempt for the establishment in all its forms: — he didn't marry, for example, and wouldn't walk arm-in-arm with his girlfriend; he didn't wear a collar and tie and refused to carry an umbrella; he scorned work, helped the underdog, smoked hashish, bitterly hated the police, and considered going to jail a mark of honor. This behavior was conspicuous in a society where everyone married, where a man worked hard fulfilling his duty to his family, and where everyone respected the basic laws and code of behavior.

It seems the *rebetes* first made their appearance a little after 1821, when Greece won its independence from the Ottoman Empire. What is now known as modern Greece had been under Turkish rule for 400 years, and during this time was made up of villages, towns, and small ports. In the years that followed independence, Greece began to industrialize, the cities and ports grew in size, and both the bourgeois class and the underworld increased in numbers. Athens is an outstanding example of this urban growth. In 1834, when it became the capital of the small Greek kingdom, it had about 10,000 inhabitants. In 1848 it had 26,000 and the total population of Greece was 987,000. Subsequently Athens grew to 43,000 in 1861; 63,000 in 1879; 107,000 in 1889; and 167,000 in 1907. By 1920 it had reached 285,000 and by 1928 453,000; In the beginning of the 1970's greater Athens approached 3 million while the entire population of Greece had risen to 9 million, which means that by then one-third of the population lived in greater Athens.

During this period of time, specifically the latter part of

the 19th century, the *manges/rebetes* of the underworld were developing their own way of life. They frequented specific neighborhoods: — in Athens for example, one of their areas was Psyrri, near the markets; among their districts in Piraeus were Karaiskaki and Trouba; and in Thessaloniki, Vardari was a favorite hangout. In these neighborhoods they had their own *tavernas* and cafes, they controlled smuggling, the hashish market, the gambling clubs and the whorehouses, and trafficked in stolen goods. The *rebetes* always had their own style of dress. In the later evolution of the style the *rebetis* wore tight trousers made of the best imported material, a dark collarless shirt usually black or purple, narrow pointed shoes with high heels, and a fedora hat pushed far back on his head, or so far forward that he had to tilt his head back to see. The hat had a black band to show mourning for his victims. He carried a knife or revolver in his belt and in his hand a cane made of hard cherry wood which he could use as a weapon in fights. He wore his jacket with only the left arm in the sleeve so that he could flip it round the forearm as a shield against his opponent's knife or cane. He walked with a subtly arrogant swagger, left shoulder hunched slightly forward to keep his jacket on, often playing a *komboloi*, and swinging only his right hand. In the early days the *rebetis* wore a long wide sash of silk or wool wound tightly around his waist with the ends hanging free. The folds of cloth at his waist served as a carrier for all his goods — tobacco, money, knives and revolvers; and anyone who stepped on the sash ends that he purposely dragged on the ground was asking for a fight.

During this same period the *rebetes* greased their hair to form a series of curls on their foreheads, and waxed their moustaches. They painted beauty marks on their faces, allowing a few facial hairs to grow at that spot to add authenticity to the mark, and they painted their eyes with black shadow to produce an elongated effect.

The *manges* trusted only *manges* and avoided dealings with other persons. The police persecuted them as an objectionable social element, and the upper and middle classes ignored them and wished they didn't exist. Their moral isolation was so complete that no Greek writer wrote about them except in terms of curses and condemnation. The Greek political Left also denounced them, even more strongly than the police, and although some articles have emerged from the Left in the late sixties and early seventies, these articles have arbitrarily approved or condemned the songs on the basis of their political applicability.

The *rebetic* songs are the most accessible source of information about the life and attitudes of the *rebetes*. They contain a variety of themes: love, poverty, jail, the underworld, death, hashish, etc., but about half the songs are concerned with love, particularly lost love and unrequited love. An important characteristic of these songs is that dance is an integral element along with the music and lyrics, and it must be considered as such. Equally important is the language. The *rebetes* spoke and still speak their own argot, which is exceptionally rich in expressions and hand gestures. The songs draw both from this argot as well as from the language of the working class Greeks, and it is this mixed language that constitutes the poetic expression of *rebetika*.

The womb of *rebetika* was the jail and hashhouse. It was there that the early *rebetes* created their songs. They sang in quiet, hoarse voices, unforced, one after the other, each singer adding a verse which often bore no relation to the previous verse, and a song often went on for hours. There was no refrain, and the melody was simple and easy. One *rebetis* accompanied the singer with a *bouzouki* or *baglamas*, and perhaps another, moved by the music, would get up and dance. The early *rebetic* songs, particularly the love songs, were based on Greek folk songs and the songs of the Greeks of Izmir and Istanbul. In 1922, one and a half million Greek refugees from Asia Minor, largely destitute, flooded into Greece. They constituted approximately one-quarter of the total population then, and the people who settled in the urban areas had a strong influence on *rebetika*. Among the characteristics of this period of creativity, which lasted roughly until 1932, were the use of the *outi* and *santouri* as accompanying musical instruments, and a predominance of songs delivered in a slow wailing vocal style. In the following decade, the 'classical' period of *rebetika*, the *bouzouki*, especially under the influence of the great composer and performer Markos Vamvakaris, became the chief musical instrument. Other important figures of this period were Batis, Papaioannou, Stratos, Tountas. From 1940 to 1952, which was the last creative period of *rebetika*, the main force behind the composition of the songs was Vasilis Tsitsanis, who abandoned the old instruments and concentrated on the *bouzouki* and a younger generation of singers. Mitsakis and Khiotis were also big names during this time.

In the 1930's a good number of *rebetika* were recorded in Greece on 78 RPM discs and were quite successful. It should be noted, however, that from 1936 until today, without interruption, all recordings have had to pass through a government censorship office. This of course meant that alterations often had to be made in the original song texts, as for example in the case of the songs referring to hash. Moreover, studio recording and the fixed time limit of the record itself imposed an artificiality on the free expression of the songs. At the same time, fame and money began to corrupt the composers and singers. During the Axis occupation of World War II no *rebetika* were recorded. After the war rapid systematic commercialization begins to take place: the old composers and lyric writers disappear, whereas the singers are idolized. After 1955, with the mass production of long play records in Greece, the *rebetic* song is virtually lost. The underworld is no longer involved, the orchestra embellishes the music, the themes become insipid and artificial, and the places where the songs are played are now the most expensive nightclubs in Greece.

Research on *rebetika* hasn't yet begun. This research should center first of all on the collection and preservation of relevant documents. These should be examined by a wide range of specialists who can compare them with similar songs in other societies. Next, social scientists and historians need to study the birthplace of the *rebetika*, the jails

and hashhouses. Then hopefully we can get a better picture of how and why the *rebetes* actually came into existence.*
The argot of the underworld should be studied, and the enormous influence the Turkish culture had in forming the modern Greek society must be taken into consideration. Above all it must be recognized that *rebetika* are one of the most important expressions of modern Greece, and no one interested in the life and culture of its people can afford to overlook them.

Elias Petropoulos

* Since this article was written, a lot of research on *rebetika* has indeed taken place in Greece, much of it by Elias Petropoulos himself. In addition to academic research, the topic has since been dealt with in many forms of the arts, including painting, literature, theater and cinema.

A bouzouki player

The Music of the Rebetes

The traditional music of Greece is one branch of what is generally called Near and Middle Eastern music. Until the Middle Ages a large part of the East and West shared many of the same musical traditions. There are still relics of these common traditions in West and North European folk music. For example, compare this line from a Greek folk song (Bourgault-Ducoudray, *Trente Melodies Populaires de Grèce et d'Orient*, Paris 1876, p. 78):

with the following line from a Hebridean folk song (M. Kennedy - Fraser, *Songs of the Hebrides*, II, London 1917, p. xxi):

Also compare the following two examples:

From a Norwegian folk song (*Norsk Folke Musikk*, RCA FEP 6, US 1175):

From a Greek folk song (G. Pakhtikos, *260 Δημώδη Ελλη-νικά Άσματα*, Athens 1905, p. 7):

But towards the end of the Middle Ages we find an increasingly wide divergence between the mentality of Western and Eastern musicians. Western music began building itself on different concepts while Eastern music, including that of Greece, retained its old musical traditions. The Western composer, advancing with his culture upwards through levels of increasing sophistication and correlative personal isolation, perceives himself increasingly as an individual and expresses his own personal feelings through the music. The Eastern musician, as in all more archaic societies, considers himself not as a separate individual, but as a member of the group, a part of the whole. Correspondingly, he uses an accumulation of modes and melodic patterns known by the group to fashion music which expresses the feelings of the group and which is within the accepted tradition.

Within this overall music tradition — but exclusive of what is called in Greece 'serious' and 'light' music, and which is, with a few exceptions in the area of *avant garde* music, largely imitative of European classical or light music — there are three basic types of music in Greece today. There is Byzantine or church music, which is supervised by the clergy. Here the composer confines himself to a rather strict tradition in order to create a certain atmosphere desired by the church. Second, there is a vast body of folk music, which is the music of the villages. And then there is urban music, which falls into two categories, the *rebetic* and the popular. The latter includes some interesting original music based mainly on traditional themes (e.g. Mikis Theodorakis), but also a lot of pseudo-folk and pseudo-*rebetic* commercial music with no particular aesthetic value.

Until the late 19th Century the difference between the music liked in the Greek countryside and that liked in the towns was slight. The town music of this period employed more or less the same scales and rhythms as the corresponding folk music, though in general it could be described as having a greater degree of variety, complexity and sophistication.

Rebetic music sprang out of the town music, probably in the early 20th century. Its creators, the *rebetes*, were simply villagers who had left their homes and were trying to make a living in the developing ports and industrial towns. Although they continued to maintain close contact with the members of their own group, these *rebetes* began to reveal, from their perspective on the fringes of this new urban society, the first signs and symptoms of individualization. There is a new flavor in this music, which became better defined and more independent in style as it became more conscious of itself. By 1930 to 1935, this very special and unmistakable *rebetic* music was reaching its full expression, which at its culmination (1935-50) was so vital and effective that all popular urban music written in Greece since about 1950 has fallen under its spell.

An examination of a fair proportion of the many thousands of pieces of *rebetic* music which were recorded on gramophone records from as early as the beginning of the 20th century shows that most of this music is vocal and dominated by the heavy and austere *Zeybekiko* rhythm and the sometimes slow and whimsical, sometimes quick and exhuberant *Khasapiko*, the two most cherished dances of the *rebetes*.

In the earlier examples (1900-30) the music is usually accompanied by small instrumental ensembles consisting of a violin, a struck dulcimer (*santouri*), and/or a guitar. The subsequent development of the *rebetic* orchestra is roughly the following: — Around 1930 the combination of violin-*santouri*-guitar began to be replaced by a *bouzouki* (an instrument like a long-necked mandolin), a guitar, and perhaps a *baglamas* (a mini-*bouzouki*). The wood of the guitar was sometimes hit when the musician wanted an occasional percussive effect. Later a second *bouzouki* was added as well as an accordion or a piano, or instead of a piano, a *santouri* or a *kanoni* (zither). The tendency to make the orchestra bigger continued, and in the early 1960's the best known creator-performer of this music had an ensemble of at least 2 *bouzoukis*, 2 *baglamades*, 2 guitars, a doublebass, a set of drums, a piano, and an electronic harmonium.

The role played by the instruments in *rebetic* music is of primary importance. First they establish the general characteristics of the given mode by playing an introduction called *taxim* with rapid notes in free rhythm, such as the following example from a *Zeybekiko* by Mitsakis («Ψιλή βροχούλα έπιασε», Columbia CG 2120):

This is usually performed by the leading soloist on the *bouzouki*. Second. they state the instrumental refrain, which may or may not be thematically related to the vocal part. And finally, they accompany the singer or singers with simple but well chosen and sometimes quite interesting chordal progressions. It should be noted in passing that the *bouzouki* rose to the peak of its popularity only in recent years, thanks to the *rebetes*. However it had been known to the Greeks for many centuries, and its original form, which was called the *pandoùra* or *pandouris*, seems to be of ancient Greek origin. Regarding its use in folk music, we know from General Kasomoulis (1792-1872) that it was very popular among the Klephts, who were guerilla fighters for the liberation of Greece from the Ottoman Turks.

The vocal part in *rebetic* music can be performed by one or more singers, but rarely more than four. This part is often divided into the song and the refrain. The song is usually sung by the leading singer and the refrain by all the singers together in unison or parallel thirds, sixths, or octaves, or even more complicated chordal formations such as triads.

In some rare cases the vocal part is sung from the very beginning alternately by two singers or by the leading singer and a small chorus which repeats the phrase, as in the following example from a *Khasapiko* by Tsitsanis (*Rebetika Songs Sung by Sotiria Bellou*, Lyra 3248, Side B, track 5):

The chief characteristics of *rebetic* music and the features that distinguish it from folk music are the timbre of the *bouzouki, baglamas* and the accordion; the chords produced by the guitar and the *baglamas*, and the parallel thirds and sixths produced by the first and second *bouzoukis* in the instrumental refrains and the singers in the vocal refrains; and the unique vocal style of the *rebetes*. Differences between the styles of folk and *rebetic* music also exist in their modal conception, formal structure, and melodic range. In *rebetic* music we seem to find a greater mixture of traditional modes and a greater variety of thematic material within the same piece, and consequently a smaller degree of repetition than exists in folk music. Also, the range of the *rebetic* songs in most cases surpasses the four to six notes of the average folk song, and in hundreds of cases it even extends beyond the usual octave.

With regard to the specific origins of *rebetic* music, the style and spirit of "The Dance of the Jew" by Neuseidler (1508/9-1563) clearly has certain characteristics in common with *rebetic* music in spite of the fact that its melody has been tonally distorted for satirical purposes:

From "*Der Judentanz*" by Neuseidler (Davidson-Apel *Historical Anthology of Music*, I, Harvard 1964, p. 108):

From a *Khasapiko* by Vamvakaris («Αλανιάρα απ' τον Πειραία», Odeon GO 2384):

From a *Zeybekiko* by Vamvakaris («Ψεύτικος ντουνιάς» Odeon GO 4033):

This supports the belief that much of the melodic material which characterizes *rebetic* music is not only of very old origin, but also belongs to the musical tradition which is shared by a considerable number of Middle Eastern people (Greeks, Jews, Turks, Arabs, etc.), But more specifically *rebetic* music seems to derive from Byzantine church music and Greek folk music. The influence of Byzantine music can be seen clearly in the following examples.

From the Ode to the Patriarch of Constantinople Eugene II, by Gregory Protopsaltis (d. 1822). (*Σύνοψις Καλοφωνικών Ειρμών*, Constantinople 1842, p. 243):

From a *Zeybekiko* by Kaldaras («Νύχτωσε χωρίς φεγγάρι», Odeon GO 3752):

From a *Doxastikon* for the Feast of St John the Baptist (Aug. 29) (*Δοξαστάριον Πέτρου*, Bucharest 1820, p. 237):

From a *Zeybekiko* by Mitsakis («Ψιλή βροχούλα έπιασε», Columbia CG 2120):

The type of folk music which exerted the strongest influence on *rebetic* music is that which was primarily played along the coasts and off-shore islands of Western Asia Minor, and particularly on the island of Lesvos. In the following example we have an old folk song from Skopelos (North Aegean) which is strikingly similar to a rebetic song by Dragatsis. From a folk song recorded in 1967 on Skopelos by the writer, sung by Diamantoula Kekhrioti:

From a *Zeybekiko* by Dragatsis («Ειρηνάκι», Odeon 190401b):

Of course as we advance in time we find elements of the modern era creeping into the music, such as certain characteristics of the French *café chantant* and music hall styles, and a particular Italian flavored type of song known as the *cantada* and sung mainly in the Ionian islands. We find this occasionally in the Khasapiko, as may be seen in the final cadence of the following example from a *Khasapiko* by Tsitsanis («Μια νύχτα στο Πασαλιμάνι», Odeon 275155b):

but not in the *Zeybekiko*, which is not so receptive to influences outside the tradition. We find it also in those *rebetic* songs which depart entirely from these two traditional *rebetic* rhythms, as in the next example, which is from a waltz by A. Khadzikhristos («Ας μη ξημέρωνε ποτέ», *Ρεμπέτικα για 6*, Margophone 8051, Side A, track 3):

Finally, some of the pieces belonging to the body of *rebetic* music are not original creations but slightly modified and sometimes differently worded versions of existing folk songs or popular hits, a fact which is clearly illustrated in the following examples.

From an island folk song notated and published by P. Philanthidis in *Phorminx*, Period II, Vol.V, No.1, Athens 1910, p. 40:

From an *allegro* by Tsitsanis («Βάρκα γιαλό», Columbia DG 6599):

From an instrumental *Zeybekiko* from Cyprus (Rickey Holden and Mary Vouras, *Greek Folk Dances*, Newark 1965, p. 120):

From a *Zeybekiko*, composer unknown («Οι νέοι χασικλήδες», Odeon A 190173a):

By 1950 to 1955 most of the best *rebetic* music had already been produced, and with few exceptions everything afterwards has merely been a variation or an imitation of old themes. Or worse, we now find a commercially successful exploitation of the old *rebetic* music forms deprived of their intimate style and spirit; and this exploitation is on such a grand scale that any further development of the music is no longer possible. The decadent post 1950-55 *rebetic* music can be recognised by the following characteristics: use of the extended orchestras described above; use of electric *bouzouki* with four instead of the traditional three courses of strings in pairs; tendency of singers to renounce the style of their predecessors, who sang in strict time, in favor of slurring the beat, which gives a sugary oversentimental flavor to the melody; tendency of singers to introduce capricious mispronunciations of the text, and to show off their vocal virtuosity.

But the old genuine *rebetic* music is unique. With the single exception of jazz, the modern world from Greece westward has not produced anything which so convincingly and authentically expresses the soul of simple people and their yearnings. When you hear this music you feel that something very deep and important is taking place, that you are encountering one of the great achievements of the human heart.

Markos Dragoumis

The Dances of the Rebetes

Another time, when my child died, I got up and danced.
The others said "Zorba's gone mad." But I knew that if I didn't
dance at that moment I would go mad.

from *Zorba the Greek*
by Nikos Kazantzakis

As with Zorba, so too with the *rebetes*. For the *rebetes*, dance
was not merely an enjoyable form of self-expression, but
often a means of hanging onto identity and sanity in a world
that appeared to hold nothing but suffering and depriva-
tion. One cannot, then. speak of their songs without also
implying dance, for dance is as central and inseparable a
part of this music as the lyrics and melodies themselves are.

The two dances of the *rebetes* are the *Zeybekiko* and the
Khasapiko. Two other dances less commonly found in
places where they gathered are the *Tsiphte Teli* and the *Karsilama*, both popularized by the *rebetes* from Anatolia in

1922 but never achieving the wide circulation of the other two. All these dances were formerly classified as couple or group folk dances, and are still found in their original demotic form and style in many non-urban areas of Greece. However, the gradual urbanization of these dances resulted in considerable stylistic change, so that the urban dance often bears little resemblance to the folk version.

The *Zeybekiko*

The *Zeybekiko* is unquestionably the *rebetes'* most frequent form of dance expression. The dance itself is unmistakable, but an ear untrained in Greek rhythms might find difficulty distinguishing between *Zeybekiko* and *Karsilama* music since both dances have nine counts to a measure. Although the *Zeybekiko* is generally played slower than the *Karsilama*, in 9/4 meter rather than 9/8, the two dances sometimes approach each other in tempo: a fast *Zeybekiko* 9/4 allegro and a slow *Karsilama* 9/8 adagio will have virtually the same tempo.

But the rhythmical breakdown of the two dances is somewhat different. The *Zeybekiko* is most frequently found in two rhythmical patterns. The first and by far the more popular is the *kophto* style, which creates a feeling of syncopation. The second is the *Syriano* style, the rhythm of the *vary Zeybekiko* which Markos Vamvakaris played when he first began his career.

Kophto

Syriano

Some *Zeybekiko* dances begin with an upbeat on 7, 8, 9, as for example in «Κάτω στα Λεμονάδικα» and «Στα Τρίκαλα»:

Here beats 1-6 are usually played *Kophto*, but there are some examples where beats 1-6 are played in *Syriano* style.

The urban *Zeybekiko* is highly individualistic. Of all the Greek dances it allows the dancer the greatest freedom of expression. Although there is some *Zeybekiko* music that can be danced in a humorous manner, and though it is also not unusual nowadays to see partners dancing opposite each other, or to see a woman dancing *Zeybekiko*, the popular urban *Zeybekiko* was always a man's solo dance. the expression of a mood, usually melancholic, deeply concentrated, often charged with the tension of accumulated suffering and suppressed violence.

Envision a small smoke-filled room late at night, the neighborhood hangout, a dozen or more *manges* and perhaps some of their women seated at tables around a small space for dancing. At one end of the room, or at one of the tables, are seated the musicians, apparently tuning their instruments: a *bouzouki*, a guitar, and a *baglamas*. The aimless strumming and picking gradually leads into something more recognizable — a *taxim*, an arhythmic instrumental introduction which draws the *manges*' attention. They try to follow the course of the improvised melody in their minds, murmuring satisfaction at an unexpected turn, or disappointment at the insufficient development of a theme. Gradually the *taxim* builds to a climax and the tension mounts as the rhythm of the *Zeybekiko* is introduced. Now one of the *manges* pushes back his chair and gets up. Putting his lit cigarette between his lips, eyes on the floor, body tense and slightly crouched, arms loosely out to the sides, he begins to move slowly, deliberately around some fixed imaginary point on the floor. Snapping his fingers to the rhythm, he elaborates his steps, occasionally doubling a step or holding a step for two beats, always circling round the point on the floor which is the unwavering focal center of his intense concentration, now and then breaking the heavy tension of the dance with explosive outbursts of energy as in sudden leaps, hops, turns, squats. No one else gets up to dance; it would be an insult and a trespass on his impending emotional release. Oddly enough this moment may come at any time, and he may decide to sit down again in the middle of the song; he is satisfied, he is released. No one cheers, no one claps. Perhaps another *mangas* who was able to project himself into the dancer's mood has a carafe of wine quietly sent to the man's table. But nothing more. The man danced for himself.

The next interval of strumming slowly leads into the favorite song of another patron, who may project his concentration onto a tangible object requiring physical action to overcome it, for example a bottle or glass of wine on the floor that he must drink from without using his hands; or there may be five bottles or glasses, which he must dance among without touching in addition to draining their contents. He may also use an overturned chair to balance himself on before turning it upright and sitting on it, again without using his hands; or he may tumble from one chair into another. He may dance with a bottle or glass of wine balanced on his forehead. He may lay a handkerchief on the floor and dance on it, or he may pick it up from the floor without using his hands. With his teeth he may pull out a knife thrust into the floor; he may also lift a tabls with his teeth. When he sits down he gets a rousing hand of applause; this was more in the nature of physical release.

A mangas dancing the Zeybekiko balancing a hookah on his head.

The *Khasapiko*

Whereas the *Zeybekiko* expresses the individualism of the performer, the *Khasapiko* demonstrates his camaraderie and receptiveness: the *Khasapiko*, which has a slow or medium 2/4 or 4/4 time signature, is customarily for two, or at most three men dancing together side by side with their neighboring hands on each other's shoulders. In its original manner of execution the *Khasapiko* was improvisational based on a fundamental step, a number of well-known variations, and a couple of steps that had been worked out and practiced by the two or three very close friends. Nowadays the variations are usually called aloud by the leader, but formerly the changes of step were signaled solely by the pres-

The Khasapiko

sure of the leader's left hand on his partner's right shoulder, and required the partner's close concentration on the leader's steps. It is precisely this technique of communication that distinguishes *rebetes* dancing the *Khasapiko*; many interesting routines are performed today by talented dancers, but the routines are memorized as entire patterns and thus lack the essence of the dance which is the intimacy of communication between the dancers.

The *Khasapiko* of present-day urban Greece is now often seen as a simplified version popularly called *Syrtaki*. Although the two dances essentially use the same basic steps and variations, the styles are altogether different: whereas the *Syrtaki* is relatively loose-jointed and bouncy, and appears to be generally aimed toward spectator approval, the true *Khasapiko* is private and concentrated, as in the *Zeybekiko*, with the dancers slightly crouched and the movements close and tense, giving the impression of a coiled spring.

The *Tsiphte Teli* and the *Karsilama*

Neither the *Tsiphte Teli*, a belly dance, nor the *Karsilama* has ever enjoyed the popularity of the *Zeybekiko* and *Khasapiko* with the *rebetes*. As dance forms they both offer the dancer some relief from the tension of the other two dances, and the style of both is noticeably sexual and effeminate in comparison with the closely controlled masculine movements of the *Zeybekiko* and *Khasapiko*. They derive from a solo and couple dance tradition which was more prevalent in Asia Minor than in mainland Greece. Although they were performed to some extent by the *rebetes* who came from Asia

Minor, they were rarely used by the *rebetes* of Athens and Piraeus except as vehicles of vocal expression. It was primarily female singers who performed these dances; as a standard sequence of dance-songs an entertainer would dance a lively, then a slow *Tsiphte Teli*, and still without pause would follow it with a fast *Tsiphte Teli* or a *Karsilama*. When men danced these two dances they moved their bodies in imitation of the female entertainers, with swaying hips, rotating bellies, undulating arms, and vibrating shoulders.

The *Tsiphte Teli* is readily distinguished by its distinctive rhythm and improvised wailing melody. It has a time signature of 4/4 with the following rhythmic pattern:

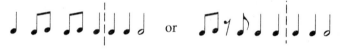

The time signature of the *Karsilama* is 9/8 (2.2.2.3) and its rhythmic pattern is:

The *Karsilama* and the *Tsiphte Teli* both are danced as solo or as couple dances, although as its name indicates, the *Karsilama* in its original demotic form is strictly a couple dance (Turk. *Karsi*=opposite, face to face; plus *lamak*= to do). Similarly, the *Tsiphte Teli* as a demotic dance can be classed as a *Karsilama*.

Ted Petrides

Rebetika and Blues

The birth and development of the Greek *rebetika* can be compared with the history of the blues, and especially the urban blues, in America. This outline locates and summarizes some of the analogies that appear to exist.

The blues is a form of music in which elements of western harmony were combined with West African musical characteristics as found in the spirituals, work songs, etc. Nevertheless, the blues remains an independent and unique musical form that was created by America's blacks.

The *rebetika* are a form of music in which elements of western harmony were combined with elements of Near Eastern music, and particularly with elements of the Greek traditional folk songs. However, the *rebetika* also retain their autonomy as a musical style.

There is no precise date for the birth of the blues, although its existence is recorded in the 19th century. Along with jazz, its diaspora from the South to the rest of the United States took place when the brothels of New Orleans were shut down by an ordinance in 1917.

The blues, and especially the urban blues, differs from folk music of the United States, although each has influenced the other.

The line of the lyrics in the blues is in iambic pentameter, a classical rhythm in poetry.

The content of the blues lyrics is chiefly erotic: disappointment in love, jealousy, desire, parting. The blues also sing about lone-

The *rebetika* seem to have existed in Greece before the Balkan Wars of 1912-13.

The refugees from Asia Minor in 1922, and especially from Constantinople (Istanbul) and Smyrna (Izmir), contributed to the spread of the *rebetika* in Greece.

The *rebetika* differ basically from Greek folk songs, even though they have been influenced by them.

In the *rebetika* the fifteen syllable line (or the eight syllable plus the seven syllable line), which is the basic rhythm in Greek poetry, is predominant.

The content of the *rebetika* is also erotic, and always heavy with bitterness. Other subjects are poverty, loneliness, social

liness, despair, misfortune, misery, social injustice, imprisonment, etc.

The blues does not bring change, does not cause revolution. is not rebellious. Its protest is stoic. Its confrontation towards the social reality is passive. This is why the younger generations of blacks, and especially the supporters of Black Power, turned away from the blues tradition to soul and free jazz.

The, blues singers were musically uneducated.

The blues was always considered to be the songs of black slaves, and of the people of the lower social levels. The whites were very slow in recognizing the blues as one of the most important forms of music ever created in the United States.

injustice, jail, *Kharos*, *tavernas*, hashish, etc.

Neither do the *rebetika* hope for social change or urge revolt. And this is why the Greek Left have ignored their existence.
It was only after 1960, when the *rebetika* were approved by the middle class and the university students, that they were accepted as songs with social content.

The creators and performers of the *rebetika* had no musical education.

The *rebetika* were considered the immoral songs of drug addicts, prisoners, the poor and uneducated. For this reason the middle and upper middle classes as well as every other form of establishment (conservatories, universities, radio and TV, and the Greek State in

The blues in its authentic form passed its creative stage around 1950.

In 1955, rock'n'roll began to conquer the white world, in and out of the United States. Rock'n'roll, which is the commercial exploitation of the blues, became fashionable and international. The blues has contributed a variety of material to pop, rock and jazz music of the last 25 years.

Just after 1960 a trend to return to the "roots" is observed in America. It has resulted in a rediscovery of the old singers and authentic blues, and in the transcription of blues songs. The whites

general) did not accept the *rebetika*, and indeed held them in contempt.

The last creative stage of the *rebetika* ends during the early 1950's.

The *rebetika* offered material to the contemporary Greek composers, who were musically educated. The *rebetika* became fashionable during the decade of the 1960's, although they never reached the disc jockeys' international Top Ten. The *rebetika* have contributed to Greek "folk pop" and popular songs, as well as to serious musical works of the last 25 years.

After 1960 the *rebetika* escape their narrow confinement and penetrate the Greek middle class. Since the late 1960's interest in *rebetika* has constantly been increasing: songs are being recorded,

in America and elsewhere have finally recognized the blues as one of the major musical forms of modem times.

independent studies are now being undertaken concerning the music and its people, and there is a growing proliferation of articles in newspapers and journals. The *rebetika* are still virtually unknown outside Greece, but within Greece a long overdue recognition of their importance is beginning to take place.

Sakis Papadimitriou

Collection of Song Lyrics

Θα σε κάνω ταίρι μου

Είμ' εργάτης τιμημένος, όπως όλ' η εργατιά,
και τεχνίτης ξακουσμένος, λεοντάρι στη δουλειά.

Εκατό δραχμές τη μέρα παίρνω, τσιβαέρι μου,
πες στη μάνα σου πως θέλω να σε κάνω ταίρι μου.

Θα σου χτίσω ένα σπίτι, γύρω με σκαλώματα,
ν' ανεβαίνεις να μου κάνεις σκέρτσα και καμώματα.

Θα μου τηγανίζεις ψάρια με πατζάρια σκορδαλιά·
θα περνάμε όλα τα βράδια με ρετσίνα και φιλιά.

Καρσιλαμάς που τραγουδούσαν οι Μικρασιάτες πρόσφυγες το 1922. Ηχογραφήθηκε αργότερα αποδιδόμενο στον Σκαρβέλη. Εκείνη την εποχή οι 100 δραχμές ήταν ένα καλό μεροκάματο. Λόγω της υψηλής ανεργίας το συνηθισμένο μεροκάματο ήταν 25 δραχμές.

I'll Make You My Mate

I'm an honest workin' man, like all the workin' class,
a legend in the trade, a lion in my work.

I make a hundred *drachs* a day, my jewel,
tell your Ma I want to make you my mate.

I'll build you a house with stairways all round
to flounce up and down and flirt and tease.

You'll fry me fish with garlic and beets,
we'll spend all the evenings with wine and kisses.

Karsilamas sung by the refugees who came to Greece from Asia
Minor in 1922. It was later recorded under the name of the composer
Skarvelis. 100 drachmas was a good daily wage. There was high un-
employment at that time and 25 drachmas was a normal daily wage.

Μαύρα μάτια, μαύρα φρύδια

Μαύρα μάτια, μαύρα φρύδια, κατσαρά μαύρα μαλλιά,
άσπρο πρόσωπο σαν κρίνο και στο μάγουλο ελιά.

Τέτιαν ομορφιά ποτές μου, αχ, τσαχπίνα μου γλυκιά,
δεν την έχω απαντήσει μέσα σ' όλο το ντουνιά.

Μαυρομάτα μου, για σένα εκατάντησα τρελός,
θα πεθάνω, δεν αντέχω, έχω μείνει ο μισός.

Πόνους έχω εγώ κρυμμένους μες στα φύλλα της καρδιάς
με τα μαγικά σου μάτια όταν, φως μου, με κοιτάς.

Χασάπικο του Μάρκου. Πρωτοηχογραφήθηκε το 1935 και ξανά το 1966.

Black Eyes, Black Eyebrows

Black eyes, black eyebrows, curly black hair,
white face like a lily and a mole on the cheek.

Such beauty, ah my sweet flirt,
I've never met in all the world.

My blackeyed one, because of you I've gone crazy,
I'll die, I can't stand it, I'm half the man I was.

I have hidden pain in the depths of my heart
when you look at me, my light, with your bewitching eyes.

Khasapiko by Markos, first recorded in 1935 and again in 1966.

«Αλήτη» μ' είπες μια βραδιά

«Αλήτη!» μ' είπες μια βραδιά, χωρίς καμιάν αιτία,
μα του αλήτη η καρδιά δε σου κρατάει κακία.

Θάρθει καιρός όμως, μικρή, να το μετανοήσεις·
για του αλήτη την καρδιά θα κλάψεις, θα δακρύσεις.

«Αλήτη» μ' είπες, μα κι εγώ χωρίς να σε μισήσω
γελώ, ακόμα κι αν πονώ, για να μη σε λυπήσω.

Ζεϊμπέκικο του Χατζηχρήστου. Πρωτοηχογραφήθηκε το 1938.

You Called Me a Bum One Night

You called me a bum one night with no reason,
but the bum doesn't bear you a grudge.

One day though, baby, you'll be sorry,
you'll cry and weep for the bum.

You called me a bum, but I don't hate you,
I laugh though it hurts so you won't be sad.

Zeybekiko by Khatzikhristos, first recorded in 1938.

Σαν μαγεμένο το μυαλό μου

Σαν μαγεμένο το μυαλό μου φτερουγίζει
κι ή κάθε σκέψις μου κοντά σου τριγυρίζει
δεν ησυχάζω και στον ύπνο που κοιμάμαι (ω)
εσένα πάντα, αρχοντοπούλα μου, θυμάμαι.

Μες στης ταβέρνας τη γωνιά για σένα πίνω,
για την αγάπη σου ποτάμια δάκρυα χύνω·
λυπήσου με, μικρή, και μη μ' αφήσεις μόνο (ω)
αφού το βλέπεις πως για σένα μαραζώνω.

Αχ, παιχνιδιάρα πάψε τώρα τα γινάτια
και μη μου κάνεις την καρδούλα μου κομμάτια
με μια ματιά σου σα μου ρίχνεις (αχ) πώς λιώνω
μαζί σου, ξέρεις, τον ξεχνάω κάθε πόνο.

Χασάπικο του Μπαγιαντέρα. Πρωτοηχογραφήθηκε το 1938 και ξανά το
1964.

My Mind as if Bewitched

My mind flutters as if bewitched
and my every thought circles round you;
I'm restless, and in my sleep when I do sleep
it's always you, little lady, I remember.

In the comer of the *taverna* it's for you I drink,
for your love I shed rivers of tears;
pity me, baby, and don't leave me lonely
since you see I'm wasting because of you.

All, little flirt, now stop being stubborn
and don't break my heart to pieces;
at one glance from you, how I melt;
with you, you know, I forget every pain.

Khasapiko by Bayianteras, first recorded in 1938 and again in 1964.

Είν' ευτυχής ο άνθρωπος

Είν' ευτυχής ο άνθρωπος π' αγάπη δε γνωρίζει
και για κοπέλες όμορφες το νου του δεν σκοτίζει.

Δεν έχει χίλιους-δυο καημούς, δεν τόνε δέρν' ο πόνος,
κι αν είναι πλούσιος ή φτωχός αυτός το ξέρει μόνος.

Έτσι κι εγώ αγάπησα κι έχω φωτιά μεγάλη·
καημούς που δεν περίμενα μου 'ρθανε στο κεφάλι.

Ζεϊμπέκικο του Τούντα. Πρωτοηχογραφήθηκε το 1939.

Lucky Is the Man

Lucky is the man that doesn't know love
and his mind's not bothered by beautiful girls.

Pain and countless sorrows don't beat on him
and he alone knows if he's rich or poor.

And that's how I too fell in love, and I'm on fire,
unexpected sorrows came down on my head.

Zeybekiko by Tountas, first recorded in 1939.

Το παλιό μου μπουζουκάκι

Το ξεκρέμασα απόψε
το παλιό μου μπουζουκάκι
για να σπάσουμε μεράκι
με μια αγάπη μου παλιά.

Το ξεκρέμασα απόψε
στο δικό της το χατίρι
κι όπως πλάι μου θα γείρει
τραγουδάκι θα της πω.

Θα της πω για την αγάπη
που 'ναι τώρα πια χαμένη
μα θα είναι ριζωμένη
όσα χρόνια κι αν θα ζω.

Πολύ αργό ζεϊμπέκικο του Χιώτη σε στίχους του Βασιλειάδη. Πρωτοηχο-
γραφήθηκε το 1946.

My Old Bouzouki

Tonight I took down
my old *bouzouki*
to have a good time
with an old love of mine.

Tonight I took it down
for her sake,
and as she leans toward me
I'll sing her a song.

I'll tell her of the love
that's already lost
but will be rooted in me
for as long as I live.

Very slow *Zeybekiko* by Khiotis with words by Vasileiadis. First
recorded in 1946.

Τ' ομορφόπαιδο

Τις λαχτάρες που μου κάνεις μη θαρρείς πως τις ξεχνώ·
κι αν γυρνάς τα βράδια μ' άλλες, βρε παλιόπαιδο,
έχε χάρη που 'σαι μάγκας κι ομορφόπαιδο.

Ό,τι μου ζητάς σ' το δίνω, σαν κορόιδο σ' αγαπώ·
κι αν μου μάσησες τα φράγκα, βρε τρελόπαιδο,
έχε χάρη που 'σαι μάγκας κι ομορφόπαιδο.

Κι όμως δεν το μετανιώνω, θέλω πίκρες να περνώ·
κι αν πεθαίνω γω για σένα, βρε τρελόπαιδο,
έχε χάρη που 'σαι μάγκας κι ομορφόπαιδο.

Ζεϊμπέκικο του Τσιτσάνη, σε στίχους του Ρούτσου. Πρωτοηχογραφήθηκε το 1948.

The Handsome Stud

The anguish you turn on in me, don't think I forget it;
but even if you fool around with others, you bastard,
I forgive you 'cause you're a *mangas* and a handsome stud.

I give you whatever you want, like a damn fool I love you;
even if you eat up my money, you nut,
I forgive you 'cause you're a *mangas* and a handsome stud.

But I don't regret it, I can take the bad times;
even if I'm dying for you, you nut,
I forgive you 'cause you're a *mangas* and a handsome stud.

Zeybekiko by Tsitsanis with words by Routsos, first recorded in 1948.

Πληροφορίες

Άσχημες πληροφορίες μου 'δωσαν για σένανε·
με τα λόγια που μου είπαν με πληγώσανε,
την καρδιά μου, σα χαρτί, την τσαλακώσανε.

Μου 'πανε το παρελθόν σου ότι είναι σκοτεινό·
ως και γράμματα μου στείλανε ανώνυμα,
από δω και πέρα, όμως, κάτσε φρόνιμα.

Ξέχασε τα περασμένα και μην τα θυμάσαι πια·
άσ' το φέρσιμο που είχες το διπρόσωπο,
κοίτα τώρα να με βγάλεις ασπροπρόσωπο.

Ζεϊμπέκικο του Τόλη Χάρμα. Πρωτοηχογραφήθηκε το 1948 και έγινε μεγάλη επιτυχία.

Information

They gave me dirty information about you;
with the things they said they hurt me,
they crumpled my heart like paper.

They told me that your past is dark,
and they still send me anonymous letters;
from now on, though, behave yourself.

Forget the past and don't dwell on it anymore;
cut out the two-faced behavior you had,
take care now not to shame me.

Zeybekiko by Tolis Kharmas, first recorded in 1948. It was a big hit of the time.

Στρώσε μου να κοιμηθώ

Πήρα τη στράτα κι έρχομαι
μες στη βροχή και βρέχομαι·
στα σκαλοπάτια σου εγώ σφυρίζω,
άσε με μέσα για να μπω
     και στρώσε μου να κοιμηθώ.

Να με στεγνώσεις με φιλιά
μες στη ζεστή σου αγκαλιά
και μη μ' αφήσεις πια να ξαναφύγω·
κοντά σου πάρε με να ζω
     και στρώσε μου να κοιμηθώ.

Κανένα μάτι δε θα δει,
πέτα σαν πρώτα το κλειδί·
κι έχεις το λόγο μου, γλυκιά μ' αγάπη,
στιγμή δε θα σ' απαρνηθώ·
     και στρώσε μου να κοιμηθώ.

Ζεϊμπέκικο του Τσιτσάνη σε στίχους του ίδιου και της Παπαγιαννοπούλου. Πρωτοηχογραφήθηκε το 1950.

Make the Bed for Me to Sleep

I took to the road and I'm coming
in the rain and I'm drenched;
at your steps I whistle,
let me come in
>   And make the bed for me to sleep.

Dry me with kisses
in the warmth of your embrace
and don't let me leave again;
take me to live with you
>   And make the bed for me to sleep.

No eye will see,
throw down the key as before;
and you have my word, my sweet love,
I'll never forsake you,
>   And make the bed for me to sleep.

Zeybekiko by Tsitsanis, words by Tsitsanis and Papaiannopoulou.
First recorded in 1950.

Η γάτα

Έδιωξα κι εγώ μια γάτα
που 'χε γαλανά τα μάτια·
σαν κοιμόμουνα τη νύχτα
μου 'χωνε βαθιά τα νύχια.

Τόσους μήνες που την είχα
μου ξηγιότανε στην τρίχα,
τώρα έγινε από σόι
και τα ψάρια δεν τα τρώει.

Τηνε διώχνω με γινάτι
και την άλλη μέρα νάτη·
μου 'ρχεται με ποντικάκια
και μου κάνει κορδελάκια.

Τώρα βρήκα άλλη γάτα,
πιο όμορφη και μαυρομάτα·
πονηρή κι αυτή, σαν γάτα,
μου τα σπάει κρυφά τα πιάτα.

Χασάπικο του Δελιά σε στίχους του Μάθεση. Είχε γραφτεί για μια ιερό-
δουλη στον Πειραιά και πρωτοηχογραφήθηκε το 1936.

The Cat

I kicked out a cat
that had blue eyes;
when I was sleeping at night
she buried her claws in me.

All the months I had her
she never did no wrong;
now she's putting on airs
and won't even eat fish.

I throw her out relentlessly
and next day here she is again;
she comes to me with mice
and plays up to me.

Now I found another cat,
more beautiful and black-eyed;
this one's tricky too, like a cat,
she sneaks in and breaks my plates.

Khasapiko by Delias with words by Mathesis, written about a prosti-
tute in Piraeus. First recorded in 1936.

Μια Κυριακή σε γνώρισα

Μια Κυριακή σε γνώρισα, καθόσουν σ' έναν πάγκο,
και στοίχημα στην τσέπη σου αν είχες ένα φράγκο.

Θυμάσαι εκείνο τον καιρό φιλιά και καρδιοχτύπια·
μαζί με την αγάπη σου πόσα φαρμάκια ήπια.

Τώρα σε βλέπω κι έρχεσαι απ' τη γωνιά του δρόμου
και σχίζεται η καρδούλα μου και χάνω το μυαλό μου.

Χασάπικο του Τσιτσάνη. Πρωτοηχογραφήθηκε το 1938.

One Sunday I Met You

One Sunday I met you, you were sitting on a bench,
and I bet you didn't have a penny in your pocket.

Remember that time, the kisses and pounding hearts?—
how much poison I swallowed along with your love.

Now I watch you coming from the street corner
and my poor heart breaks and I lose my mind.

Khasapiko by Tsitsanis, first recorded in 1938.

Το καφενεδάκι

Από τότε που 'χεις φύγει είναι όλα σκοτεινά,
κι η καρδιά μου μαύρες ώρες απ' τη θλίψη της περνά.

Για παρηγοριά μου μένει, η καρδιά μου να ξεχνά,
το μικρό καφενεδάκι, π' ανταμώναμε συχνά.

Κάθομαι στο τραπεζάκι, η αγάπη ξαναζεί,
και θαρρώ αυτές τις ώρες πως βρισκόμαστε μαζί.

Ζεϊμπέκικο του Μαρκέα και του Μάνεση. Πρωτοηχογραφήθηκε το 1946.
Η εικόνα που περιγράφει θυμίζει στίχους του Καβάφη.

The Small Café

Since you've been gone everything is dark
and my heart is going through black hours of grief.

The comfort left me, for my heart to forget,
is the small café where we often met.

I sit at the little table, love lives again,
and I imagine these hours that we're together.

Zeybekiko by Markeas and Manesis, first recorded in 1946. The imagery is reminiscent of Cavafy.

Πρωτοβρόχια

Είχες φύγει τον Απρίλη
και μονάχος είχα μείνει.

Κι ήρθες τώρα με τα πρωτοβρόχια
γιατί σ' έπιασε η φτώχια.

Τόσες μήνες λαχταρούσα
να σε δω· μα δεν μπορούσα

Ήρθες τώρα π' άρχισε να βρέχει
και το κεραμίδι τρέχει.

Ζεϊμπέκικο του Μητσάκη που γράφτηκε τον Ιούνιο του 1948 και πρωτοηχογραφήθηκε τον Δεκέμβριο του ίδιου χρόνου.

First Rain

You left in April
and I was alone.

Now you came with autumn's first rain
because poverty caught up with you.

For months I was longing
to see you, but couldn't.

You came now that it started to rain
and the roof tiles are dripping.

Zeybekiko by Mitsakis, written in June 1948 and first recorded in December 1948.

Κάνε υπομονή

Μην απελπίζεσαι και δε θ' αργήσει·
κοντά σου θα 'ρθει μια χαραυγή
καινούργια αγάπη να σου ζητήσει·
κάνε λιγάκι υπομονή.

Διώξε τα σύννεφα απ' την καρδιά σου
και με το κλάμα μην ξαγρυπνάς·
τι κι αν δεν βρίσκεται στην αγκαλιά σου;
Θα 'ρθει μια μέρα· μην το ξεχνάς.

Γλυκοχαράματα θα σε ξυπνήσει
κι ο έρωτάς σας θ' αναστηθεί·
καινούργια αγάπη θα ξαναζήσει·
κάνε λιγάκι υπομονή.

Ζεϊμπέκικο του Τσιτσάνη. Πρωτοηχογραφήθηκε το 1948 και οι στίχοι
αποδίδονται στην Παπαγιαννοπούλου.

Have Patience

Don't despair, he won't be long;
he'll come to you one dawn
asking for new love;
have a little patience.

Chase the clouds from your heart
and don't lie awake crying;
so what if he's not in your arms!
He'll come one day, don't forget it.

Some sweet dawn he'll wake you
and desire will be reborn;
new love will live again;
have a little patience.

Zeybekiko by Tsitsanis, with words attributed to Papaiannopoulou.
First recorded in 1948.

Το γράμμα

Έχω να λάβω γράμμα σου σαράντα μέρες τώρα·
τάχα να ζεις ή χάθηκες σαν το πουλί στην μπόρα;

Μέρα και νύχτα ξάγρυπνη, με μάτι δακρυσμένο,
τον ταχυδρόμο να φανεί στην στράτα περιμένω.

Σωστός αιώνας φαίνεται σε μένα κάθε ώρα·
έχω να λάβω γράμμα σου σαράντα μέρες τώρα.

Άλλοι μου λέν πως πέθανες, κι άλλοι πως ζεις για μένα,
κι άλλοι πως μ' απαρνήθηκες και πάν' όλα χαμένα.

Ζεϊμπέκικο του Τσιτσάνη. Πρωτοηχογραφήθηκε το 1948.

The Letter

I haven't had a letter from you for forty days now;
are you living, or lost like the bird in the storm?

Day and sleepless night, with tearful eye,
I wait for the mailman to come down the lane.

Each hour seems an eternity to me;
I haven't had a letter from you for forty days now.

Some tell me you died, and some that you live for me,
and others that you've forsaken me and everything is lost.

Zeybekiko by Tsitsanis, first recorded in 1948.

Κλαμένη ήρθες μια βραδιά

Κλαμένη ήρθες μια βραδιά
μες στης ταβέρνας τη γωνιά·
μα είναι αργά πολύ να ζωντανέψεις
τον έρωτα που σκότωσες.

Δε σε προσέχω σ' ό,τι λες·
δε με πειράζει· τι κι αν κλαις;
Μήπως κι εγώ για σε δεν έχω κλάψει;
Κι εσύ γελούσες, πονηρή.

Μην περιμένεις τώρα πια
να ξαναζήσουν τα παλιά·
όλα τελειώσανε πια μεταξύ μας
και δεν υπάρχει τίποτα.

Ζεϊμπέκικο του Τσιτσάνη. Πρωτοηχογραφήθηκε το 1949.

You Came Crying One Evening

You came crying one evening
to my corner in the *taverna*;
but it's too late to bring back
the love you killed.

It's nothing to me, whatever you say,
I don't care; so what if you cry! —
you think I haven't cried for you? —
and you were laughing, you bitch.

Don't wait any longer
for the past to live again;
every thing's finished with us
and nothing's left.

Zeybekiko by Tsitsanis, first recorded in 1949.

Χωρίσαμε ένα δειλινό

Χωρίσαμ' ένα δειλινό με δάκρυα στα μάτια·
η αγάπη μας ήταν γραφτό να γίνει δυο κομμάτια.

Πονώ σα συλλογίζομαι τα όμορφα τα βράδια,
που μου 'δινες, γλυκά γλυκά, όρκους, φιλιά και χάδια.

Με μια λαχτάρα καρτερώ και πόνο στην καρδιά μου,
ίσως γυρίσεις γρήγορα ξανά στην αγκαλιά μου.

Ζεϊμπέκικο του Τσιτσάνη σε στίχους του Γκούβερη. Γράφτηκε το 1943 στη μνήμη μιας εβραιοπούλας που χάθηκε στους θαλάμους αερίων. Πρωτοηχογραφήθηκε το 1949.

We Parted One Twilight

We parted one twilight with tears in our eyes;
our love was fated to become two pieces.

I ache when I think of the beautiful evenings
when you tenderly gave me promises, kisses, caresses.

With longing and pain in my heart I wait,
maybe you'll return again quickly to my arms.

Zeybekiko by Tsitsanis with verses by Gouveris. Written in 1943 in
memory of a Jewess whom the Germans took off to the gas cham-
bers. First recorded in 1949.

Αραμπάς περνά

Αραμπάς περνά·
η σατράπισσα
που αγάπησα
είναι μέσα —
αγκαλιάζεται
κι ούτε νιάζεται
η μπαμπέσα.

Αραμπάς περνά
με τη βλάμισσα
που χαράμισα
τη ζωή μου —
με ρεστάρησε,
στραπατσάρησε
το τσαρδί μου.

Αραμπάς περνά
(ω, μανούλα μου)
η καρδούλα μου
πώς χτυπάει —
η σατράπισσα
που αγάπησα
μ' άλλον πάει.

Χασάπικο του Τσιτσάνη. Πρωτοηχογραφήθηκε το 1949.

The Carriage Passes

The carriage passes;
the little tyrant
I loved
is inside
in another's arms
and doesn't even care,
the traitor.

The carriage passes
with the chick
I wasted
my life on —
she ruined me,
smashed up
my shack.

The carriage passes;
oh, Momma,
my poor heart
how it pounds —
the little tyrant
I loved
is with another guy.

Khasapiko by Tsitsanis, first recorded in 1949.

Αντιλαλούνε τα βουνά

Αντιλαλούνε τα βουνά
σαν κλαίω εγώ τα δειλινά.
Περνούν οι ώρες θλιβερές
σ' ένα παλιό ρολόι
κι εγώ τους αναστεναγμούς
τους παίζω κομπολόι.

    Αντιλαλούνε τα βουνά
    σαν κλαίω εγώ τα δειλινά.

Εμπάφιασα απ' τα ντέρτια μου
κι απ' τα πολλά σεκλέτια μου.
Κουράγιο είχα στη ζωή
μα τώρα που σε χάνω
θα ήταν προτιμότερο
για μένα να πεθάνω.

Μουγκρίζω απ' τις λαβωματιές
κι απ' τις δικές σου μαχαιριές.
Λαβωματιές με γέμισες
και μ' έφαγαν οι πόνοι
και στη φωτιά που μ' έριξες
τίποτα δε με σώνει.

Ζεϊμπέκικο του Τσιτσάνη σε στίχους της Παπαγιαννοπούλου. Πρωτοηχογραφήθηκε το 1952.

The Mountains Re-echo

The mountains re-echo
when I cry at dusk.
The sad hours tick by
on an old clock
and I play a *komboloi*
of sighs.

> The mountains re-echo
> when I cry at dusk.

I'm sick of my longing
and my endless torments.
I had courage in life
but now that I'm losing you
it would be better
for me to die.

I'm groaning from wounds
and the stabs of your knife,
I'm full of wounds
and pains have devoured me,
and in the fire where you threw me
nothing can save me.

Zeybekiko by Tsitsanis with words by Papaiannopoulou, first recorded
in 1952.

Στον Πειραιά συννέφιασε

Ανάβω το τσιγάρο μου και η βροχή το σβήνει·
χτυπώ την πόρτα π' αγαπώ και κείνη δεν ανοίγει.

Στον Πειραιά συννέφιασε και στην Αθήνα βρέχει
άλλος αγάπη έχασε κι άλλος αγάπη έχει.

Βλέπω τις κούρσες να περνούν απ' το μεγάλο δρόμο
και συ (το ξέρω) πως γελάς με το δικό μου πόνο.

Σε μια κολόνα στέκομαι και πήρε να νυχτώνει·
δεν λογαριάζω την βροχή όσο κι αν δυναμώνει.

Ζεϊμπέκικο του Μητσάκη. Πρωτοηχογραφήθηκε το 1960.

In Piraeus It's Cloudy

I light my cigarette and the rain puts it out;
I knock on the door I love and it doesn't open.

In Piraeus it's cloudy and in Athens it's raining;
one guy lost love and another guy has love.

I see fancy cars passing on the avenue
and I know you're laughing at my pain.

I'm standing by a lamppost and it's getting dark;
I don't give a damn for the rain, let it pour.

Zeybekiko by Mitsakis, first recorded in 1960.

Το πορτοφόλι

Στον κόσμο το σημερινό, αυτό το ξέρουν όλοι,
η δύναμη στον άνθρωπο είναι το πορτοφόλι.

Σαν πορτοφόλι μάθουνε πως έχεις μες στην τσέπη
σε λεν πως είσαι τζέντελμαν, πως είσαι καθώς πρέπει.

Το πορτοφόλι (τι τα θες;) έχει μεγάλη χάρη·
σε κάθε δύσκολη στιγμή σε βγάζει παλικάρι.

Ζεϊμπέκικο του Περιστέρη. Πρωτοηχογραφήθηκε το 1938 και ξανά το 1964.

The Wallet

In the world today, as everybody knows,
a man's strength is his wallet.

When they learn you've got a wallet in your pocket
they say you're a gentleman, you're really okay.

But what do you expect, the wallet's a winner;
in every tight spot you come out a *palikari*.

Zeybekiko by Peristeris, first recorded in 1938 and again in 1964.

Συννεφιασμένη Κυριακή

Συννεφιασμένη Κυριακή, μοιάζεις με την καρδιά μου,
που έχει πάντα συννεφιά, Χριστέ και Παναγιά μου.

Είσαι μια μέρα σαν κι αυτή που 'χασα τη χαρά μου·
συννεφιασμένη Κυριακή, ματώνεις την καρδιά μου.

Όταν σε βλέπω βροχερή, στιγμή δεν ησυχάζω·
μαύρη μου κάνεις τη ζωή και βαριαναστενάζω.

Ζεϊμπέκικο του Τσιτσάνη σε στίχους του Γκούβερη. Γράφτηκε το 1943 και
πρωτοηχογραφήθηκε το 1948. Ένα από τα πιο αγαπημένα ρεμπέτικα.

Cloudy Sunday

Cloudy Sunday, you're like my heart
that's always cloudy, Christ and the Holy Virgin.

You're a day like the when one I lost my joy;
cloudy Sunday, you make my heart bleed.

When I see you rainy I can't get a moment's peace;
you make my life black and I sigh heavily.

Zeybekiko by Tsitsanis, words by Gouveris. Written in 1943, first
recorded in 1948. One of the best loved *rebetic* songs.

Μεσάνυχτα

Μες στα βαθιά μεσάνυχτα χτυπάει το ρολόι
κι εγώ στους δρόμους τραγουδώ το ντέρτι που με τρώει.

Με απορία με κοιτούν τη νύχτα οι διαβάτες,
που σαν κουρέλι περπατώ στις έρημες τις στράτες.

Πονώ και μες στη μοναξιά ο ύπνος μου με τρώει
και στα βαθιά μεσάνυχτα χτυπάει το ρολόι.

Ζεϊμπέκικο του Βασιλειάδη. Πρωτοηχογραφήθηκε το 1947.

Midnight

In the depths of midnight the clock strikes
and I sing on the streets of the woe that gnaws at me.

The people passing in the night look at me in wonder
as I walk the deserted streets like a rag.

I suffer and in the loneliness my sleep gnaws at me,
and in the depths of midnight the clock strikes.

Zeybekiko by Vasileiadis, first recorded in 1947.

Πάνω σ' ένα βράχο

Σ' ένα βράχο φαγωμένο από κύμα αγριωπό
ένα σούρουπο είχα κάτσει λίγο να συλλογιστώ.

Κάθε βήμα στη ζωή μου είναι πόνος και συμφορά·
θέλω ο δόλιος να πετάξω μα δεν έχω τα φτερά.

Έτσι μ' έχει καταντήσει μιας γυναίκας η οργή·
στρώμα να 'χω τα χορτάρια και προσκέφαλο τη γη.

Ζεϊμπέκικο του Καλδάρα. Πρωτοηχογραφήθηκε το 1948.

On a Rock

On a rock eaten away by fierce waves
I sat awhile one twilight to reflect.

Each step in my life is pain and disaster;
heartsick I would fly, but I have no wings.

A woman's rage has left me with
weeds for my bed and the ground as a pillow.

Zeybekiko by Kaldaras, first recorded in 1948.

Ένας διαβάτης

Αυτό το βράδυ το σκοτεινό
είμαι μονάχος και σε ζητώ·
πού να γυρίζεις, που να γλεντάς,
με ποιον τα πίνεις και με ξεχνάς;

Με πνίγει απόψε η ερημιά
και παίρνω σβάρνα τα καπηλιά·
γυρνώ στους δρόμους εδώ κι εκεί
κανείς δεν ξέρει πού να 'σαι συ.

Ένας διαβάτης είμαι κι εγώ
χωρίς να ξέρω για πού τραβώ·
δίχως ελπίδα μες στην καρδιά
ψάχνω για να 'βρω παρηγοριά.

Ζεϊμπέκικο του Τζουανάκου. Πρωτοηχογραφήθηκε το 1949.

A Man on the Streets

This dark night
I'm alone and I want you;
where do you hang out, where do you live it up,
who do you drink with and forget me?

Tonight loneliness is strangling me,
and I comb the cheap *tavernas*,
I trudge the streets here and there,
no one knows where you are.

I'm just another man on the streets,
without knowing where I'm headed,
without hope in my heart,
searching for consolation.

Zeybekiko by Tzouanakos, first recorded in 1949.

Γράμμα θα στείλω στον Θεό

Γράμμα θα στείλω στον Θεό με λόγια πικραμένα,
να του μιλήσω να σκεφτεί λιγάκι και για μένα.

Ας λένε πως δεν χάνει κανέναν ο Θεός·
μ' αδίκησε ο κόσμος, με ξέχασε κι αυτός.

Θα του μιλήσω όμορφα, ντόμπρα, παλικαρίσια·
όταν μοιράζει τον παρά να τον μοιράζει ίσια.

Γράμμα θα στείλω στον Θεό για να με συγχωρήσει·
δεν πρέπει στο παράπονο κι εμένα να μ' αφήσει.

Ζεϊμπέκικο του Μπαμπάκη. Πρωτοηχογραφήθηκε το 1950.

I'm Going to Send God a Letter

I'm going to send God a letter with bitter words
to tell Him to think a little about me too.

> Let them say God doesn't forsake anyone,
> but the world did me wrong and He forgot me too.

I' ll talk to Him nice and straight and bold;
When He hands out the bread He should divide it up fair.

I'm going to send God a letter to spare me,
He shouldn't leave me with this gripe.

Zeybekiko by Babakis, first recorded in 1950.

Καημός

Ηλιοβασίλεμα σωστό των ώρα που νυχτώνει·
τραβώ σκυφτός το δρόμο μου, καημός με μαραζώνει.

Γκρίζα γινήκαν τα μαλλιά, λύγισε το κορμί μου,
και το μαράζι ρίζωσε βαθιά μες στην ψυχή μου.

Πόνοι με δέρνουνε πολλοί, καημοί με βασανίζουν,
και κάθε μέρα που περνά τα νιάτα μου τσακίζουν.

Ζεϊμπέκικο του Λαύκα σε στίχους του Βασιλειάδη. Πρωτοηχογραφήθηκε το 1951.

Despair

The sun really sets the hour when night falls;
bowed down I go my way, despair consumes me.

My hair's turned gray, my body's bent,
and gloom's rooted deep in my soul.

Endless torments beat me down, despair racks me,
and every passing day destroys my youth.

Zeybekiko by Lafkas, with words by Vasileiadis. First recorded in 1951.

Μουρμούρικο

Ήσουνα (τι ήσουνα;) μια παξιμαδοκλέφτρα
και τώρα που σε πήρα γω γυρεύεις σούρτα-φέρτα.

Βρε, ήσουνα ξυπόλητη και γύριζες στους δρόμους
και τώρα που σε πήρα γω γυρεύεις ιπποκόμους.

Ήσουνα ξυπόλητη και μάζευες ραδίκια
και τώρα που σε πήρα γω γυρεύεις βαντανίκια.

Ήσουνα ξυπόλητη και πάταγες στις λάσπες
και τώρα που σε πήρα γω γυρεύεις άσπρες κάλτσες.

Ήσουνα ξυπόλητη και τάιζες κοκόρους
και τώρα που σε πήρα γω ζητάς αεροπόρους.

Ήσουνα ξυπόλητη και μάζευες κοσάρια
και τώρα που σε πήρα γω γυρεύεις κατοστάρια.

Πενήντα χρόνια φυλακή τιμώρησα το Χάρο
να 'σαι πάντα λεύτερη μαζί σου να γουστάρω.

Τα ζάρια μου τα κούνησα και ήρθαν έξι-πέντε
μπάνιζε μπάτσους στη γωνιά τούς πάει πέντε-πέντε.

Ζεϊμπέκικο. Τραγούδι της φυλακής που ποτέ δεν ηχογραφήθηκε σε αυτή
την εκδοχή. Άρχισε να τραγουδιέται ήδη από το 1900.

Murmuring

You were, what were you? a stale bread thief,
now that I took you in you want the good life.

Vreh, you were barefoot wandering the streets,
now that I took you in you want butlers.

You were barefoot gathering dandelions,
now that I took you in you want earrings.

You were barefoot walking in the mud,
now that I took you in you want white stockings.

You were barefoot feeding chickens,
now that I took you in you want pilots.

You were barefoot getting twenty *drachs*,
now that I took you in you want hundreds.

Fifty years in jail I cheated *Kharos*
so you'd always be free for us to make it together.

I rolled my dice and they came up six and five;
check out the cops on the corner, they're scared shitless.

Zeybekiko. A song of the jails which has never been recorded in this
version. It was being sung as early as 1900.

Κάτω στα Λεμονάδικα

Κάτω στα Λεμονάδικα έγινε φασαρία·
στα χέρια πιάστηκ' ο Θωμάς μαζί με τον Ηλία.

— Βρε συ Θωμά, μην κάνεις φασαρίες,
γιατί θα μπλέξεις άσχημα και θα 'χεις ιστορίες.

Κάτω στα Λεμονάδικα έγινε φασαρία·
δυο λαχανάδες πιάσανε και κάναν την κυρία.

— Κυρ-αστυνόμε, μη βαράς, γιατί κι εσύ το ξέρεις,
πως η δουλειά μας είν' αυτή και ρέφα μη γυρεύεις.

Ζεϊμπέκικο άγνωστου συνθέτη. Το τραγουδούσε ο υπόκοσμος στη διάρκεια της δεκαετίας του 1920. Λεμονάδικα ονομαζόταν μια περιοχή της προκυμαίας του Πειραιά (σημερινή πλατεία Καραϊσκάκη).

Down in Lemonadika

Down in Lemonadika there was trouble;
Thomas and Elias knocked each other around.

"*Vreh* Thomas, don't make trouble,
you'll get tangled in a mess and have problems."

Down in Lemonadika there was trouble;
two pickpockets they grabbed played it straight.

"Officer, don't beat us, because you know it too,
that this is our work, and no kick-back's due."

Zeybekiko by an unknown composer. It was sung in the underworld during the 1920's. Lemonadika was the name of a dock area in Piraeus.

Η ντερμπεντέρισσα

Τρέξε, μάγκα, να ρωτήσεις να σου πουν ποια είμαι γω·
είμαι γω γυναίκα φίνα, ντερμπεντέρισσα,
που τους άντρες σαν τα ζάρια τους μπεγλέρισα.

Δε με συγκινούν αγάπες φτάνει να καλοπερνώ·
κάθε βράδυ να τραβάω το ποτήρι μου
και να σφάζονται λεβέντες για χατίρι μου.

Πως θα γίνω γω δική σου, πάψε να το συζητάς·
δε γουστάρω τις παρόλες, σου ξηγήθηκα,
στις ταβέρνες και στα καμπαρέ γεννήθηκα.

Ζεϊμπέκικο του Τσιτσάνη σε στίχους του Ρούτσου. Πρωτοηχογραφήθηκε το 1949. Ντερμπεντέρισσα αποκαλούσαν οι μάγκες έναν συγκεκριμένο τύπο γυναίκας που ανήκε στον κόσμο τους και διέθετε ιδιαίτερα χαρακτηριστικά, τα οποία θαύμαζαν: ήταν ανεξάρτητη και συχνά με έντονη θηλυκότητα. Αγαπούσε τη ζωή και ζούσε για τη στιγμή. Δεν έκανε μόνιμους δεσμούς και ήταν περίπου το αντίθετο της συμβατικής γυναίκας της παραδοσιακής ελληνικής κοινωνίας.

The Derbederissa

Run, *mangas*, ask them to tell you who I am;
I'm a fine tough woman, a *derbederissa*,
I've played men like dice.

Love doesn't stir me, I just want a good time,
to get my drinks every night
while he-men fight over me.

That I'll be yours, shut up about it;
I don't dig sweet talk, I've made that clear;
I was born in the *tavernas* and cabarets.

Zeybekiko by Tsitsanis with words by Routsos. First recorded in 1949.
Derbederissa is a term the *manges* used for a certain type of woman
who belonged to their world and who possessed specific qualities
which they admired: she was tough and independent and often in-
tensely feminine, she loved life and lived in the moment, she made
no permanent attachments, and was virtually the antithesis of the
conventional woman in the traditional Greek society.

Είμαι πρεζάκιας

Είμαι πρεζάκιας, μάθε το, κι όπου κι αν θα πάω
ο κόσμος μ' αποστρέφεται, δεν ξέρω τι να κάνω.

Τα ρούχα μου ελιώσανε, φάνηκε το κορμί μου·
η πρέζα μου κατάστρεψε τέλεια τη ζωή μου.

Σ' ένα βαγόνι κάθομαι και σπίτι δεν θυμάμαι·
ένα τσουβάλι βρώμικο το στρώνω και κοιμάμαι.

Με βλέπουν και σιχαίνονται, μα γω δυάρα δεν δίνω·
την πρέζα μόνο θα τραβώ κι ό,τι μου μέλλει ας γίνω.

Σαν αποθάνω, φίλε μου, έρχετ' η αστυνομία·
με κάρο σκουπιδιάρικο μου κάνουν την κηδεία.

Σαν μαστουριάσω, φίλε μου, δική μου η Αθήνα·
είμαι πρεζάκιας, μάθε το, δεν ξέρω τι να κάνω.

Χασάπικο του Τσαούση σε στίχους αγνώστου, που τραγουδιόταν από τη
δεκαετία του 1930.

I'm a Junkie

I'm a junkie, see, and wherever I go
they shit on me, I don't know what to do.

My clothes are rags, nothing but holes,
junk completely wrecked me.

l live in a freight car and don't remember home,
a burlap sack is where I sleep.

When they see me they puke, but I don't give a damn,
junk's my whole life, whatever will be will be.

The police are coming when I die, my friend,
with a garbage cart for a hearse.

But when I get down, friend, all Athens is mine;
I'm a junkie, see, I don't know what to do.

Khasapiko by Tsaousis with words by an unknown writer. It was
being sung since the 1930's.

Από τότε που άρχισα

Απ' τον καιρό που άρχισα την πρέζα να φουμάρω
ο κόσμος μ' απαρνήθηκε, δεν ξέρω τι να κάνω.

Απ' τις μυτιές που τράβαγα άρχισα και βελόνι
και το κορμί μου άρχισε σιγά-σιγά να λιώνει.

Τίποτε δεν μ' απόμεινε στον κόσμο για να κάνω,
αφού η πρέζα μ' έκανε στους δρόμους να πεθάνω.

Χασάπικο του Κωστή. Πρωτοηχογραφήθηκε το 1910 (;) και ξανά το 1934
από τον Δελιά.

From the Time I Began

From the time I began to snort smack
the world turned away, I don't know what to do.

The junk I sniffed started me on the needle
and slowly my body began to waste.

Nothing in the world was left for me to do
after smack drove me out on the streets to die.

Khasapiko by Kostis, first recorded in 1910(?). Recorded again in
1934 by Delias.

Ο μαθητής

Μ' έστειλε η μανούλα μου σκολιό για να πηγαίνω,
μα γω τραβούσα στο βουνό με μάγκες να φουμέρνω.

Με μάλωνε ο δάσκαλος γράμματα για να μάθω
κι εγώ απ' τη μαστούρα μου δεν έβλεπα να γράφω.

Μη με βαράς, κυρ-δάσκαλε, και μη μου κάνεις κόλπα
και δε μαθαίνω γράμματα τόσες φορές σου το 'πα.

Αντί σκολιό εγώ τράβαγα για του Καραϊσκάκη,
έπινα διάφορα ποτά για να γενώ μαγκάκι.

Ζεϊμπέκικο του Μάρκου Βαμβακάρη. Πρωτοηχογραφήθηκε το 1936. Στην περιοχή Καραϊσκάκη του Πειραιά σύχναζαν οι μάγκες.

The Pupil

Poor Ma would send me off to school,
but I'd head for the hill to smoke with the *manges*.

The teacher was riding me to learn my lessons
and I was so high I couldn't see to write.

"Don't beat me, Teacher, and don't try to con me,
I'm not going to study, I told you a million times."

Instead of school I'd head for Karaiskaki
and drink like mad trying to be a little *mangas*.

Zeybekiko by Markos, first recorded in 1936. Karaiskaki is a neighborhood in Piraeus which was frequented by *manges*.

Βαρέθηκα τον αργιλέ

Βαρέθηκα τον αργιλέ, σιχάθηκα τη μαύρη·
θ' αφήσω το κορμάκι μου άλλους νταλκάδες να 'βρει.

Τις όμορφες θα κυνηγώ, κρασί και σαντουράκι,
κι όχι το παλιομπούζουκο και το μπαγλαμαδάκι.

Φύγε από με κουτόχορτο, χάσου κι εσύ τσιμπούκι,
ν' ανοίξω τα ματάκια μου από το μαστουρλούκι.

Γιατί σαν τη φουμάριζα έπεφτα και στο ζάρι,
κι άλλοι μ' έλεγαν έξυπνο και άλλοι παλαβιάρη.

Ζεϊμπέκικο του Χρυσούλη. Πρωτοηχογραφήθηκε το 1938.

I'm Fed Up with the Hookah

I'm fed up with the hookah, I'm sick of black hash;
I'm going to let my poor body find other passions.

I'll hunt beautiful girls, wine and the *santouri*,
and not the no-good *bouzouki* and the *baglamas*.

Split, stupid spice, you too, hookah,
so I can see my way out of the high.

Because when I smoked I took to the dice,
and some said I was smart, and others called me crazy.

Zeybekiko by Khrisoulis, first recorded in 1938.

Λιτανεία

Σαν χριστιανός ορθόδοξος, σ' αυτήν την κοινωνία,
εβάλθηκα, ρε μάγκες μου, να κάνω λιτανεία.

Ψωνίζω τις τζουρίτσες μου κι ένα κομμάτι μαύρο
και ξεκινώ, ρε μάγκες μου, να πάω στον Άγιο Μάμα.

Μπαίνω μέσα στην εκκλησιά, στις στρογγυλές καμάρες,
κι αρχινώ τις τσιμπουκιές, σαν νάτανε λαμπάδες.

Κι ο αρχάγγελος αποκεί με μια μεγάλη φούρια
απ' τα ντουμάνια τα πολλά τον έπιασε μαστούρα.

Μου λέει· άκου, χριστιανέ, δεν είναι αμαρτία,
που μπήκες μες στην εκκλησιά να κάνεις λιτανεία.

Μα ξάφνου κι ένας καλόγερος μου λέει· τράβα πίσω,
γιατί κι εγώ έχω σειρά, καμιά για να ρουφήξω.

Ζεϊμπέκικο του Τσιτσάνη που γράφτηκε το 1942. Τραγουδιόταν σπάνια
και δεν ηχογραφήθηκε ποτέ στην Ελλάδα. Ο Άγιος Μάμας είναι χωριό
στη Χαλκιδική.

Litany

Like an Orthodox Christian in this society
I was set, *vreh manges*, to say the litany.

I go to get roaches and a piece of black hash
and I set out, *vreh manges*, to go to St. Mamas.

I go into the church, into the rounded arches,
and get going on the pipes as if they were candles.

And from in there the archangel, all in a rush
— from the thick smoke a high caught him —

He tells me, "Listen Christian, it's no sin
that you came in the church to say the litany."

But suddenly a monk too tells me, "Get in line,
because it's my turn to have a drag."

Zeybekiko by Tsitsanis, written in 1942. Rarely sung, and has never been recorded in Greece. St. Mamas is a village in Chalkidiki, near Thessaloniki.

Η δροσούλα

Άνω-κάτω χτες τα κάνανε
στου Σιδέρη τον παλιό τεκέ·
πρωί-πρωί με τη δροσούλα,
απάνω στη γλυκιά μαστούρα,
στήσανε καβγά δυο μάγκες
για να κάνουν ματσαράγκες.

Τεκετζή μου, βάστα να σου πω,
σου μιλάει ο μάγκας με καημό,
το χασίσι κι αν φουμάρω
εγώ κανένα δεν πειράζω·
είμαι μάγκας και αλάνης
κι ήρθα στον τεκέ χαρμάνης.

Μπήκα μόνος μέσα στον τεκέ
να φουμάρω έναν αργιλέ,
να φουμάρω, να μπαφιάσω,
και τις πίκρες να ξεχάσω·
μες στην τόση μου σκοτούρα
βρίσκω γλέντι στη μαστούρα.

Ζεϊμπέκικο του Τσιτσάνη που γράφτηκε το 1944 και πρωτοηχογραφήθηκε
το 1946. Ο Σιδέρης ήταν αληθινό πρόσωπο, ένας ευγενικός άνθρωπος χα-
μηλών τόνων που είχε χασισοποτείο στη Θεσσαλονίκη. Πέθανε το 1966.

The Dew

They turned it all upside down yesterday
at Sideris' old hash den;
early in the morning with the dew,
at the peak of a sweet high,
two *manges* setup a row
so they could make some scores.

"Hash den owner, hold on, I'll tell you,"
the *mangas* speaks to you in sorrow,
"even when I smoke hash
I don't hassle anyone;
I'm a *mangas* and a guy from the streets
and I came to the hash den with a craving.

"I came in the hash den alone
to smoke a hookah,
to smoke, to get mellowed out
and forget my troubles;
in the midst of so much worry
I find kicks in getting stoned."

Zeybekiko by Tsitsanis written in 1944 and first recorded in 1946.
Sideris was a real person, a kind soft-spoken man who had a hash
den in Thessaloniki. He died in 1966.

Ο λουλάς

Όταν καπνίζει ο λουλάς
εσύ δεν πρέπει να μιλάς·
κοίταξε τριγύρω, οι μάγκες
κάνουν όλοι τουμπεκί.

Άκου που παίζει ο μπαγλαμάς
και πάτα αργιλέ για μας·
σαν θα γίνουμε μαστούρια
θα 'μαστε προσεκτικοί.

Κανένα μάτι μη μας δει
και μας μπλοκάρουν, δηλαδή,
και μας βρούνε καμιάν αιτία
και μας πάνε όλους φυλακή.

Ζεϊμπέκικο του Μητσάκη. Πρωτοηχογραφήθηκε το 1946. Το τραγούδι απευθύνεται σ' έναν πρωτάρη χασισοπότη ο οποίος έρχεται για πρώτη φορά στον τεκέ και παίρνει οδηγίες για τον απαραίτητο κώδικα συμπεριφοράς.

The Bowl

When the bowl's being smoked
you mustn't speak;
look around, the *manges*
all keep their silent cool.

Listen to the *baglamas*
and stoke the pipe for us;
when we get stoned
we're going to watch out.

No one should see us
and hem us in,
or find some excuse
and take us all to jail.

Zeybekiko by Mitsakis, first recorded in 1946. The song is directed
to a novice hash smoker who has been brought into the hash den
for the first time. He is being instructed in the requisite code of behavior.

Ο ισοβίτης

Στη φυλακή με βάλανε ισόβια για σένα·
τέτοιον μεγάλονε καημό υπόφερα για σένα.

Εσύ 'σαι η αιτία του κακού για να με τυρανούνε,
οι πίκρες και τα βάσανα να με κρυφογερνούνε.

Εφτά φορές ισόβια με πάν να με δικάσουν
και στην κρεμάλα τ' Αναπλιού εκεί να με κρεμάσουν

Συνήγορους και δικαστές τους πλάνεψε η ομορφιά σου
και με δικάζουνε ισόβια για να γενεί η καρδιά σου.

Τώρα θα κάνω έφεση, ίσως με βγάλουν όξω,
κακούργα, δολοφόνισσα, για να σε πετσοκόψω.

Απ' τη ραδιουργία σου μπουζούριασα το χύτη,
χωρίς να θέλω μ' έκανες να γίνω ισοβίτης.

Θα σου 'ριχνα πετρέλαιο κι ύστερα να σε κάψω
και μες στο ξεροπήγαδο θα πά' να σε πετάξω.

Και μια μεγάλη εγδίκηση, σαν τηνε ξεμπουκάρω·
όπως τον Έκτωρ ο Αχιλλεύ τον έσερνε στο κάρο.

Χασάπικο του Μάρκου Βαμβακάρη σε στίχους αγνώστου. Πρωτοηχογραφήθηκε το 1936.

The Lifer

They threw me in jail for life because of you;
I've been suffering such terrible grief because of you.

They're tormenting me for the trouble you caused;
the sorrows and trials are gnawing away my youth.

Seven times they take me to send me up for life
and string me up on the gallows of Nafplion.

Your beauty seduced the lawyers and judges
and they send me up for life to make you happy.

Now I'm going to make an appeal, maybe they'll let me out,
you criminal, you murderess, so I can hack you to pieces.

From your plotting I knocked off the steelworker,
without me wanting it you made me a lifer.

I'd pour gasoline on you and then burn you
and go throw you in the dried up well.

What sweet revenge, when I break out of here,
like Achilles dragged Hector with his cart.

Khasapiko by Markos with words by an unknown writer, first
recorded in 1936.

Νύχτωσε χωρίς φεγγάρι

Νύχτωσε χωρίς φεγγάρι· το σκοτάδ' είναι βαθύ·
κι όμως ένα παλικάρι δεν μπορεί να κοιμηθεί.

Άραγε τι περιμένει, όλη νύχτα ως το πρωί,
στο στενό το παραθύρι που φωτίζει το κελί;

Πόρτ' ανοίγει – πόρτα κλείνει, μα διπλό 'ναι το κλειδί·
τ' έχει κάνει και το ρίξαν το παιδί στη φυλακή;

Πόρτ' ανοίγει – πόρτα κλείνει με βαρύ αναστεναγμό·
ας μπορούσα να μαντέψω της καρδιάς του τον καημό.

Ζεϊμπέκικο του Καλδάρα που γράφτηκε για έναν πολιτικό κρατούμενο την εποχή του Ελληνικού Εμφυλίου (1946-49). Πρωτοηχογραφήθηκε το 1947 και ξανά το 1963.

Night Is Fallen without a Moon

Night is fallen without a moon; the darkness is deep;
yet a *palikari* can't sleep.

Wonder what he's waiting for all night long
by the narrow window that lights the cell.

A door opens – a door closes, but the key is turned twice;
what's the kid done that they threw him in jail?

A door opens – a door closes with a heavy groan;
if only I could guess the sorrow of his heart.

Zeybekiko by Kaldaras, written about a political prisoner at the time
of the Greek Civil War 1946-49. First recorded in 1947, and again in
1963.

Γεντί-Κουλέ

Βράδιασε και στο Γεντί-Κουλέ,
σπάσανε τα σήμαντρα, σκοτάδι είναι βαθύ·

κάποιος όμως, κάποιος που πονάει,
δεν μπορεί να κοιμηθεί.

Έλα, μανούλα μου, πριν με δικάσουνε
κλάψε να μ' απαλλάξουνε.

Δεν είναι το σφάλμα μου βαρύ·
βαριά όμως τα σίδερα βαριά κι η φυλακή·
είναι πόνος, πόνος και μαράζι,
αδικία να σε βρει.

Βράδιασε μες στο Γεντί-Κουλέ,
ο κόσμος έξω χαίρεται την όμορφη ζωή
κι εγώ στενάζω, στενάζω νύχτα-μέρα
μέσα δω στη φυλακή.

Ζεϊμπέκικο του Μητσάκη. Πρωτοηχογραφήθηκε το 1957. Το Γεντί-Κουλέ, στη Θεσσαλονίκη, λειτουργούσε ως φυλακή μέχρι το 1989.

Gedi-Koulé

Night is fallen even at Gedi-Koulé,
the prison bells are hushed, darkness is deep;
but someone, someone who's suffering
can't sleep.

> Come on Mama, before they try me,
> cry, so they'll let me go.

My crime isn't harsh,
but the chains are harsh, harsh too the prison;
it's pain, pain and wasting
when injustice strikes you.

Night is fallen inside Gedi-Koulé,
the world outside's celebrating the good life,
and I sigh, I sigh night and day
here inside the prison.

Zeybekiko by Mitsakis, first recorded in 1957. Gedi-Koulé was a barbaric prison in Thessaloniki which functioned until 1989.

Φτώχια

Δεν με φόβισαν κύματα, χιόνια κι ανεμοβρόχια,
όσο με φόβισες εσύ, καταραμένη φτώχια.

Απ' τα φτωχά μου όνειρα ένα σωστό δεν βγαίνει,
όλα τα σκόρπισες εσύ, φτώχια καταραμένη.

Στον έρωτα και στη ζωή, όπου και να με νιώσεις,
φτώχια, δεν πέρασε στιγμή χωρίς να με πληγώσεις.

Ζεϊμπέκικο του Χατζηχρήστου. Πρωτοηχογραφήθηκε το 1939.

Poverty

Waves, snow, and storms never scared me
as much as you did, damned poverty.

Not one of my poor dreams is coming true,
you scattered them all, damned poverty.

Wherever you noticed me in love and in life
you never once failed to wound me, poverty.

Zeybekiko by Khatzikhristos, first recorded in 1939.

Το σβηστό φανάρι

Κατ' απ' το σβηστό φανάρι
κοιμάται κάποιο παλικάρι·
με δίχως φράγκο μες στην τσέπη
τι όνειρο άραγε να βλέπει;

Ξένος όπου κι αν γυρίζει,
όποια πόρτα κι αν χτυπήσει·
δεν έχει μάνα να πηγαίνει
τα ρούχα του, τουλάχιστο, να πλένει.

Έχει σπίτι το σβηστό φανάρι
και για λάμπα το φεγγάρι·
κι εσείς, διαβάτες που περνάτε,
τον ύπνο του να μην του τον χαλάτε.

Ζεϊμπέκικο του Μητσάκη. Πρωτοηχογραφήθηκε το 1949.

The Unlit Streetlamp

Under the unlit streetlamp
some *palikari*'s sleeping
without a penny in his pocket;
I wonder what he's dreaming.

A stranger wherever he roams,
whatever door he knocks on;
he's got no mama to go to,
not even to wash his clothes.

His home's the unlit streetlamp
and for a light he has the moon;
you people who pass by,
don't disturb his sleep.

Zeybekiko by Mitsakis, first recorded in 1949.

Το κρεβάτι του πόνου

Μες στο κρεβάτι του πόνου
κυλιέμαι χρόνια χωρίς γιατριά·
μπροστά μου βλέπω τον θάνατό μου,
νέους και νέες μας έκανε στοιχιά.

Πονεί το στήθος μου, γλυκιά μου μάνα,
νιώθω να σκίζεται το κορμί,
πέφτουν τα φύλλα, χτυπάει η καμπάνα,
πλακώνει η νύχτα μαύρη, σκοτεινή.

Πες μου, βρε μάνα, ποια τιμωρία
χωρίς συμπόνια με τυραννά·
ίσως δική σου να 'ν' αμαρτία
κι ούτε ο Χάρος δε με συμπονά.

Μες στο κρεβάτι αυτό του πόνου
το Χάρο να 'ρθει παρακαλώ,
να με γλιτώσει, γλυκιά μου μάνα,
απ' το μαρτύριο τούτο το κρυφό.

Ζεϊμπέκικο του Τσιτσάνη. Πρωτοηχογραφήθηκε το 1949. Στην Ελλάδα, μέχρι τα μέσα του 20ού αιώνα η φυματίωση μάστιζε τα αστικά κέντρα. Οι ασθενείς στιγματίζονταν, όπως περίπου συνέβαινε στις ΗΠΑ μέχρι πρόσφατα με τους καρκινοπαθείς και τους ψυχασθενείς. Γι' αυτό τόσο οι ίδιοι όσο και οι οικογένειές τους προσπαθούσαν να το κρύψουν.

The Bed of Pain

In this bed of pain
I've tossed years without a cure;
before me I see my death,
when we're young it makes us ghosts.

My chest hurts, sweet Mom,
I feel like my body's tearing apart,
the leaves are falling, the bell's tolling,
night's blowing in, black and dreary.

Tell me, *vreh* Mom, what punishment
tyrannizes me without pity?
maybe it's because of your own sins
that even *Kharos* shows me no pity.

In this bed of pain
I beg *Kharos* to come
and deliver me, sweet Mom,
from this hidden martyrdom.

Zeybekiko by Tsitsanis, first recorded in 1949. Until the middle of the 20th century pulmonary tuberculosis was the prevalent urban disease in Greece. It carried a stigma similar to that formerly attached to cancer and insanity in the United States, and victims of the illness and their families tried to keep it secret.

Τον Χάρο τον αντάμωσαν

Τον Χάρο τον αντάμωσαν πεντέξι χασικλήδες
να τον ρωτήσουν πώς περνούν στον Άδη οι μερακλήδες.
Πες μας, βρε Χάρε, να χαρείς το μαύρο σου σκοτάδι·
έχουν τάλιρα, έχουν ρακί, να πίνεται στον Άδη;
Πες μας αν έχουν μπαγλαμά, μπουζούκια, και γλεντάνε·
βρίσκουνε κόλπα, έχουν τσαρδί, πού παν και ξενυχτάνε;
Πες μας αν έχουν γκόμενες, μανίτσες, και γουστάρουν,
και τσιγαράκι σέρτικο με κέφι να φουμάρουν.
Πες μας, βρε Χάρε, να χαρείς· τι κάνουνε τ' αλάνια;
Στον Κάτω Κόσμο πίνουνε ή κάθονται χαρμάνια;
Κι όσοι από καρασεβντά επήγανε στον Άδη,
πες μας αν γιατρευτήκανε ή λιώσαν στο σκοτάδι.
Πιάσε δυο δράμια προυσαλιό και πέντε μυρωδάτο
και δώσε να φουμάρουνε τ' αδέρφια εκεί κάτω.

Το τραγούδι έχει έντονες ομοιότητες με αντίστοιχα δημοτικά. Οι ρεμπέτες
το τραγουδούσαν ήδη από τη δεκαετία του 1920. Απαντάται σε πολλές
εκδοχές. Στις πρώιμες μορφές του ήταν χασάπικο, μετά έγινε ζεϊμπέκικο.

They Met Kharos

Five or six hash smokers met up with *Kharos*
to ask him how the guys who love life make out in Hades.
Tell us, *vreh Kharos* — may you enjoy your black darkness —
do they have dough? do they have *raki* to drink in Hades?
Tell us if they have *bouzouki*s and *baglamas* to live it up.
Can they hustle? do they have joints to hang out in all night?
Tell us if they have women, sweet mamas to make it with
and hash cigarettes to smoke in a good mood.
Tell us, *vreh Kharos* — may you have joy — what do the
        bums do?
Do they drink in the Lower World and sit around talking?
And if somebody goes to Hades from heartbreak,
tell us if they get well or waste in the darkness.
Take two drams of Bursa hash and five of the scented mix
and give it to our brothers to smoke down below.

This song has strong resemblances to analogous Greek folk songs.
The *rebetes* were singing it since the 1920's. It exists in many versions.
In its earlier forms it was a *Khasapiko*, later a *Zeybekiko*.

Η ξενιτιά

Με γέρασε η ξενιτιά και τρώει τη ζωή μου·
δεν την αντέχω, μάνα μου, φθείρεται το κορμί μου.

Η ξενιτιά έχει καημούς, έχει πολλά φαρμάκια·
παίρνει παιδάκια απ' τη ζωή και λιώνει τα κορμάκια.

Θα φύγω, μάνα, δεν μπορώ· κοντά σου θα γυρίσω
κι απ' τον καημό της ξενιτιάς, μάνα μου, να γλιστρήσω.

Μα μια γυναίκα γνώρισα, εδώ στα ξένα που 'μαι·
θα τήνε πάρω, μάνα μου, μαζί κι οι τρεις να ζούμε.

Ζεϊμπέκικο του Καλδάρα. Πρωτοηχογραφήθηκε το 1947. Ο τελευταίος στίχος δεν είχε συμπεριληφθεί στην ηχογράφηση. Το τραγούδι μιλάει για τον ξενιτεμό, σύνηθες φαινόμενο για τους νέους των φτωχών οικογενειών, που αναγκάζονταν να πάνε σε άλλες χώρες για να δουλέψουν ως ανειδίκευτοι εργάτες, με στόχο να στέλνουν χρήματα πίσω στις οικογένειές τους. Οι συνθήκες ζωής τους εκεί ήταν πολύ δύσκολες. Συντηρούνταν με τα απολύτως απαραίτητα και ονειρεύονταν την ημέρα της επιστροφής στο σπίτι τους.

This Alien Life

This alien life's making me old and eating me alive,
I can't stand it, Mom, my body's wearing out.

This alien life holds misery, it holds a lot of bitterness,
it takes kids from life and wastes their poor bodies.

I'm leaving, Mom, I can't take it; I'm returning to you
Mom, and getting out of the misery of this.alien life.

But I met a woman here in this foreign land,
I'm bringing her, Mom, all three of us will live together.

Zeybekiko by Kaldaras, first recorded in 1947. The last verse was not included on the recording. The Greek song title signifies the common practice of young men from poor families going abroad to work as unskilled laborers, specifically for the purpose of sending money back to Greece to support their families. They usually went because of dire economic need, not from choice, and it was considered a kind of living death. They maintained themselves on the barest necessities of life, and dreamt of the day when they could return home.

Όταν πίνεις στην ταβέρνα

Όταν πίνεις στην ταβέρνα κάθεσαι και δε μιλάς,
κάπου-κάπου αναστενάζεις απ' τα φύλλα της καρδιάς.

Θάθελα να σε ρωτήσω και να πληροφορηθώ·
ποιο μεράκι σ' έχει κάνει τόσο μελαγχολικό;

Μήπως έχεις αγαπήσει και προδόθηκες κι εσύ;
Έλα, κάθησε κοντά μας, να γλεντήσουμε μαζί.

Χασάπικο του Τσιτσάνη. Πρωτοηχογραφήθηκε το 1950.

When You Drink in the Taverna

When you drink in the *taverna*, you sit and don't speak,
now and then you sigh from the depths of your heart.

I'd like to ask you and find out
what longing has made you so blue.

Maybe you too have loved and were betrayed;
come sit with us and let's all have a good time.

Khasapiko by Tsitsanis, first recorded in 1950.

Απόψε κάνεις μπαμ!

Απόψε κάνεις μπαμ, απόψε κάνεις μπαμ,
σε βλέπουν και φρενάρουνε και σταματούν τα τραμ.
Κουρντίστηκες στην πένα, στο καντίνι,
να ζήσει κι ο λεβέντης που σε ντύνει—
απόψε κάνεις μπαμ.

Ξαπλώσου στο ταξί, ξαπλώσου στο ταξί,
και πάμε να γλεντήσουμε σε φίνο μαγαζί.
Απόψε στην ταβέρνα, πωπώ, τι έχει να γίνει
κι αν κάνεις πως χορέψεις ποτήρι δε θα μείνει—
απόψε κάνεις μπαμ.

Αμάν και τ' είσαι συ, αμάν και τ' είσαι συ,
για χάρη σου σταθήκανε οι άντρες προσοχή.
Απόψε σε γλεντάω κι ο κόσμος πά' να σκάσει,
κοντεύει απ' τη ζήλια να τους φύγει το καφάσι—
απόψε κάνεις μπαμ.

Ζεϊμπέκικο του Τσιτσάνη. Πρωτοηχογραφήθηκε το 1952. Ο τέταρτος στί-
χος της δεύτερης στροφής αναφέρεται στο έθιμο του σπασίματος των πιά-
των στις ταβέρνες, στα πόδια των χορευτών.

Tonight You're Dynamite

Tonight you're dynamite, tonight you're dynamite,
they see you and jam on the brakes and stop the tram.
You're decked out fit to kill, and you damn well know it,
here's to the champ who dressed you—
tonight you're dynamite.

Lean back in the taxi, lean back in the taxi,
and let's go live it up in a high class joint.
Tonight in the *taverna*, oh man, what's going to happen,
and if you get up to dance, there won't be a glass left—
tonight you're dynamite.

Wow, you're really something, wow, you're really something,
because of you the men stopped short and did a doubletake.
Tonight's on me, and the world's going to bust wide open,
they're about to blow their minds from jealousy—
tonight you're dynamite.

Zeybekiko by Tsitsanis, first recorded in 1952. The fourth line of the
second stanza refers to the custom of *taverna* patrons throwing dishes
onto the dance area to break at the feet of a dancer they admire.

Το σακάκι

Πάλιωσε το σακάκι μου·
θα σβήσω απ' το μεράκι μου·
και καημό έχω μεγάλο
δεν μπορώ να πάρω άλλο.

Πόσα κουστούμια χάρισα·
μα τώρα που ρεστάρησα
φίλος δε με πλησιάζει
τα παλιόρουχα κοιτάζει.

Ντυμένο σε προσέχουνε
κι όλοι κοντά σου τρέχουνε·
σαν παλιώσουν πέρα ως πέρα
δε σου λένε καλημέρα.

Ζεϊμπέκικο του Τσιτσάνη. Πρωτοηχογραφήθηκε το 1948.

The Jacket

My jacket's worn out,
I'm going to die of the blues;
and I'm really down,
I can't get another.

How many suits I gave away!
but now that I'm broke
not a single friend comes near;
they eye the old rags.

When you're duded up they care
and everyone flocks round,
but when all your clothes begin to fray
they don't even say hello.

Zeybekiko by Tsitsanis, first recorded in 1948.

Όσοι γινούν πρωθυπουργοί

Όσοι γινούν πρωθυπουργοί όλοι τους θα πεθάνουν·
τους κυνηγάει ο λαός απ' τα καλά που κάνουν

Απέθανε ο Κονδύλης μας, πάει κι ο Βενιζέλος,
την πούλεψε κι ο Δεμερτζής που θα 'φερνε το τέλος.

Βάζω υποψηφιότητα πρωθυπουργός να γίνω,
να κάθομαι τεμπέλικα να τρώω και να πίνω.

Και ν' ανεβαίνω στη βουλή, εγώ να τους διατάζω,
να τους πατώ τον αργιλέ και να τους μαστουριάζω.

Ζεϊμπέκικο του Μάρκου Βαμβακάρη. Πρωτοηχογραφήθηκε το 1936. Οι άντρες που αναφέρονται στο τραγούδι ήταν γνωστοί Έλληνες πολιτικοί, οι οποίοι πέθαναν όλοι στις αρχές του 1936.

Whoever Becomes Prime Minister

Whoever becomes prime minister is sure to die;
the people hunt them down for the good things they do.

Our Kondilis died and Venizelos is gone
and Demertzis vanished, who would have put things right.

I'm going to run for prime minster,
to laze around eating and drinking.

And to get up in parliament, to order them around,
to stoke their hookah and get them stoned.

Zeybekiko by Markos, first recorded in 1936. The men mentioned in
the song were prominent Greek statesmen who all died within the
early part of 1936.

Τι άλλο θέλεις;

Ήμουνα μάγκας μια φορά με φλέβ' αριστοκράτη,
τώρα θα γίνω δάσκαλος σαν το σοφό Σωκράτη.

Και Πάρις θα γινόμουνα, να 'κλεβα την Ελένη,
ν' αφήκω τον Μενέλαο με την καρδιά καμένη.

Τι άλλο θέλεις να γινώ για να με αγαπήσεις,
αφού με το κεφάλι σου τον Ξέρξη θα ζητήσεις;

Ήθελα να 'μουν Ηρακλής, όταν σε πρωτοείδα,
να σου 'κοβα την κεφαλή σαν την Λερναία Ύδρα.

Ζεϊμπέκικο του Μάρκου Βαμβακάρη. Πρωτοηχογραφήθηκε το 1935.

What Else Do You Want

Once I was a *mangas* with aristocratic blood,
now I'll become a teacher like the wise Socrates.

And I would have become Paris and stolen Helen,
to leave Meneleus with a burnt out heart.

What else do you want me to be to make you love me?
with the head you've got you're looking for Xerxes.

I wish I'd been Hercules when I first saw you,
to cut off your head like the Lernaean Hydra.

Zeybekiko by Markos, first recorded in 1935.

Το σακάκι

Η τύχη του το έφερε να κλέψει ένα σακάκι·
το πάγαινε για πούλημα μες στο Μοναστηράκι —
το πάγαινε για πούλημα να πιει κάνα κρασάκι.

Κατά κακή του σύμπτωση να και τ' αφεντικό του·
του φώναζε, του έλεγε, πως ήτανε δικό του—
του φώναζε, μα του 'λεγε, πως ήτανε δικό του.

Τον μάγκα τον τσακώσανε, τη μάπα του την πήραν,
στο ξύλο τον μουρλάνανε, στη φυλακή τον κλείσαν —
στο ξύλο τον τρελάνανε, στη φυλακή τον κλείσαν.

Μην τον βαράτε, ρε παιδιά, για 'να παλιό σακάκι·
το πάγαινε για πούλημα μες στο Μοναστηράκι —
το πάγαινε για πούλημα να πιει κάνα κρασάκι.

Ζεϊμπέκικο του Δελιά. Πρωτοηχογραφήθηκε το 1934.

The Jacket

His fate led him to steal a jacket;
he was taking it to sell in Monastiraki —
he was taking it to sell to drink a little wine.

By a stroke of bad luck there came the owner too;
he was yelling at him, saying it was his —
he was yelling at him, telling him it was his.

They busted him, the *mangas*, they took his loot;
they beat him half crazy, they locked him in jail —
they beat him half mad, they locked him in jail.

Don't beat him, you guys, for an old jacket;
he was taking it to sell in Monastiraki —
he was taking it to sell to drink a little wine.

Zeybekiko by Delias, first recorded in 1934. Monastiraki is the Athens
flea market.

Μάνα, με μαχαιρώσανε

Μάνα, με μαχαιρώσανε,
δυο μαχαιριές μου δώσανε,
αυτοί που με ζηλεύουνε
και το κακό μου θέλουνε.

Κλάψε με, μάνα, κλάψε με,
τώρα που θα πεθάνω
και να 'ρχεσαι την Κυριακή
στον τάφο μου από πάνω.

Θέλω να 'ρχόσαστε κι οι δυο,
εσύ κι ο αδερφός μου,
να κλαίτ' απαρηγόρητα
τον τζάμπα σκοτωμό μου.

Τα δυο μικρά τ' αδέρφια μου,
όταν θα μεγαλώσουν,
να πά' να βρούνε το φονιά,
και να τόνε σκοτώσουν.

Ζεϊμπέκικο του Μάρκου Βαμβακάρη βασισμένο σε αντίστοιχο δημοτικό τραγούδι. Πρωτοηχογραφήθηκε το 1936. Παραδοσιακά ο μεγαλύτερος γιος αναλαμβάνει μαζί με τον πατέρα τη συντήρηση της οικογένειας, ακόμα κι αν ο ίδιος έχει γυναίκα και παιδιά να συντηρήσει. Η οικογένεια δεν αντέχει να στερηθεί τη συνεισφορά του, οπότε — όπως δηλώνει και το τραγούδι — ο μεγαλύτερος γιος απαλλάσσεται από το καθήκον της εκδίκησης για τον φόνο και αναλαμβάνουν οι νεότεροι.

Ma, They Knifed Me

Ma, they knifed me,
they stabbed me twice,
those guys who envy me
and want the worst for me.

Cry for me, Ma, cry for me,
now that I'm going to die,
and come Sundays
to stand over my grave.

I want you both to come,
you and my brother,
to cry inconsolably
for my senseless murder.

My two little brothers,
when they grow up,
must go find the murderer
and kill him.

Zeybekiko by Markos based on an analogous Greek folk song. First recorded in 1936. Traditionally the eldest son in the family shares responsibility with the father for the family's welfare. He may himself have a wife and children to support. The family cannot afford to lose him as a provider; hence, as in this song, the duty of avenging the murder passes over the eldest remaining brother and falls on the younger ones.

Σβήσε το φως

Άσε με στη βαθιά σκοτούρα
και μην αρχίζεις την μουρμούρα·
κόφτο γαζί, μην το τραβούμε,
σβήσε το φως να κοιμηθούμε.

Μου 'χεις ζαλίσει το κεφάλι,
άσε τη γκρίνια την μεγάλη·
σαν ξημερώσει θα τα πούμε,
σβήσε το φως να κοιμηθούμε.

Έλα γλυκά και φίλησέ με,
σβήσε το φως κι αγκάλιασέ με·
με γκρίνιες άκρη δε θα βρούμε,
σβήσε το φως να κοιμηθούμε.

Χασάπικο του Παπαϊωάννου. Πρωτοηχογραφήθηκε το 1948.

Turn Off the Light

Let me alone in my deep blues
and don't get started on the nagging;
cut the jabber, let's don't drag it out,
turn off the light so we can go to sleep.

You've made my head spin,
leave off the heavy grumbling;
when day breaks we'll talk,
turn off the light so we can go to sleep.

Come and kiss me sweetly,
turn off the light and hold me in your arms;
we won't find an answer in grumbling,
turn off the light so we can go to sleep.

Khasapiko by Papaioannou, first recorded in 1948.

Κούνα, μπέμπη

Κούνα, μπέμπη, τον κεφτέ σου
να φχαριστηθεί ο τζες σου.

Κούνα, μπέμπη, τον κλανιά σου
να φχαριστηθεί η καρδιά σου.

Παλιό, αδημοσίευτο τραγούδι της φυλακής. Πρόκειται για το μόνο ομο-
φυλοφιλικό τραγούδι που προέκυψε κατά την έρευνα.

Swing, Baby

Swing your butt, baby,
to please your lover.

Swing your farter, baby,
to please your heart.

An old unpublished song from the jails. It is the only homosexual
song that has surfaced.

Musical Examples

What Else Do You Want

(See p. 146-147)

μου - να μάγ - κας μια φο - ρά με φλέβ' α - ρι - στο - κρά - τη, τώ -

ρα θα γί - νω δά - σκα - λος σαν το σο - φό Σω - κρά - τη, τώ -

ρα θα γί - νω δά - σκα - λος σαν το σο - φό Σω - κρά - τη, ή -

μου - να μάγ - κας μια φο - ρά με φλέβ' α - ρι - στο - κρά - τη.

Turn Off the Light

(See p. 152-153)

Andantino

(Bouzouki)

Α - σε με στη βα-θειά σκο - τού-ρα   και   μην αρ-

χί-ζεις τη μουρ-μού-ρα,   κόφ'   το γα - ζί μην το τρα-

βού-με,   σβύ-σε το φως να   κοι - μη - θού-με,

κόφ'   το γα - ζί μην το τρα-βου-με,

σβύ-σε το φως να   κοι - μη - θού-με.

— 159 —

You Called me a Bum One Night

(See p. 52-53)

A - λή - τη μ' εί-πες μια βρα-διά,

χω - ρίς καμ-μιά αι - τί - α,

να του α - λή - τη η καρ - διά,

δεν σου κρα-τάει κα - κί - α.

When You Drink in the Taverna (See p. 138-139)

Allegretto

(Bouzouki)

Ὅ-ταν πί-νεις στη τα - βέρ-να κά - θε-σαι και δε μι

λάς, κά-που κά-που α-να-στε - νά-ζεις απ' τα φύλ-λα της καρ

διάς, κά-που κά που α-να- στε - νά-ζεις απ' τα φύλ-λα της καρ

διάς, ό - ταν πί - νεις στη τα -

βέρ - να κά - θε - σαι και δε μι - λάς.

— 161 —

Night Is Fallen without a Moon (See p. 124-125)

Maestoso

Νύ - χτω - σε χω-ρίς φεγ-γά-ρι,   το   σκο - τά-δι 'ναι βα-θύ,

κι'ό - μως   έ - να πα - λι - κά - ρι,

δεν   μπο - ρεί να   κοι - μη - θεί,

κι'ό - - μως   έ - να πα - λι - κά - ρι,

δεν   μπο - ρεί να   κοι - μη - θεί.

We Parted One Twilight

(See p. 80-81)

Χω - ρί - σαμ' έ - να δει - λι - νό

με δά - κρυ - α στα μά - τια

κι α - γά - πη μας ή - ταν γρα - φτό,

να γί - νει δυό κομ - μά - τια

η α - γά - πη μας ή - ταν γρα - φτό

να γί - νει δυό κομ - μά - τια

Cloudy Sunday

(See p. 90-91)

Maestoso

(Bouzouki)

(Accordion)

Fine

Συν-νε-φια-σμέ - νη Κυ - ρια - κή,

μοιά - ζεις με τη καρ-διά_____μου,

που έ - χεις πάν-τα συν - νε-φιά, συν - νε - φιά,

Χρι-στέ και Πα__ Χρι-στέ και Πα-να-γιά μου,

που έ - χεις πάν-τα συν - νε-φιά, συν - νε - φιά,

Χρι-στέ και Πα__ Χρι-στέ και Πα-να-γιά μου.

The Letter

(See p. 76-77)

Allegretto

Ἔ - χω νά λά-βω γράμ-μα σου

σα-ράν-τα μέ-ρες τώ - ρα

τά-χα νά ζής ή χά - θη-κες χά - θη - κες,

σάν τό που - λί στή μπό - ρα

A fast Khasapiko

Glossary of Transliterated Words

Names of persons and places are not included. Note also that the plural transliterations of *bouzouki* and *taverna* are given the English s-plural in this book, in recognition of the fact that these two words already seem to be entering the English language.

baglamas sing. (μπαγλαμάς), *baglamades* pl. (μπαγλαμάδες) —A plucked stringed musical instrument similar to a *bouzouki* but smaller.

bouzouki (μπουζούκι) — A plucked stringed musical instrument belonging to the saz family.

cantada (καντάδα) — A serenade type song.

derbederissa (ντερμπετέρισσα) — See note to song, page 107.

drachs — Shortened from drachmas pl. (δραχμές). Standard unit of Greek currency, replaced by the Euro in 2001.

kanoni (κανόνι) — A plucked stringed musical instrument similar to a zither.

karsilama (καρσιλαμά) or *karsilamas* (καρσιλαμάς) — A medium tempo dance with nine counts to the measure. See page 39.

Kharos (Χάρος) — According to ancient legend Kharon (or Charon) was the boatman who ferried the souls of the newly dead across the River Styx to the Lower World. According to Christian tradition the soul is led before God by the Archangel Michael, who in religious paintings usually holds a broadsword in his right hand to remove the soul from a man in his death throes, and in his left a scale to weigh the sins of the freed soul. In the popular imagination the functions have been confused and combined in a modern *Kharos*, who is the personification of death. *Kharos* comes dressed in black with drawn sword to kill men and take away their souls. He is relentless and deaf to all pleas for mercy, and his coming is anticipated with fear and resignation. A clever man might be able to trick him or bargain with him, but this is rare.

khasapiko (χασάπικο) — A dance with 2/4 or 4/4 time signature. See page 37.

komboloi (κομπολόι) — A string of beads carried in the hand to toy with as a pastime.

kophto (κοφτό) — Cut. Musically, a sudden break in the line; a syncopated beat.

mangas sing. (μάγκας). *manges* pl. (μάγκες) — Member of Greek urban sub-culture designated as the underworld.

outi (ούτι) — An unfretted lute.

palikari (παλικάρι) — In former times a *palikari* was a young man who was a warrior. Nowadays the term is loosely applied to any young man with the implicit compliment that the speaker credits him as having the general attributes of a warrior.

raki (ρακί) — A hard distilled spirit.

rebetic (ρεμπέτικ/ος) — Adjective deriving from *rebetis* and transliterated from the Greek adjective stem. The Greek language uses it as a qualifying term specifically for the songs (including music and dance), and not to describe other aspects of the life of the *rebetes*.

rebetika (ρεμπέτικα) — Noun derivative from the adjective form.

rebetis sing. (ρεμπέτης), *rebetes* pl. (ρεμπέτες) — Used synonymously with *manges* in this book, although current research indicates that these words may have been used to indicate rather different types of people.

santouri (σαντούρι) — A struck stringed musical instrument similar to a dulcimer.

Syriano (συριανό) — Adjective derivative from the name of the Greek island Syros.

syrtaki (συρτάκι) — A dance resembling the *khasapiko*.

taverna (ταβέρνα) — A place where alcohol is served. *Tavernas*, open only at night, used to be the backbone of social life in Greece. Still today Greek people go to *tavernas* to spend the entire evening drinking and eating, talking and joking, often singing and dancing until the early hours of the morning. Old-time *tavernas* would serve primarily wine drawn from the barrel, the food being usually simple: a piece of grilled meat with fried potatoes and a salad, perhaps some olives, cheese and bread.

taxim (ταξίμ) — An arhythmic instrumental introduction. See page 36.

tsiphte teli (τσιφτετέλι) — A belly dance. See page 39.

vary (βαρύ/ς) — Heavy, austere, extreme.

vreh (βρε) — A familiar interjection, inadequately translatable as: "Hey!" It conveys lack of respect, and it is usually considered impolite to use it in speaking to strangers or casual acquaintances. But in the songs in this book it is used with close familiars, and the disrespect in the word is disarmed by intimacy.

zeybekiko (ζεϊμπέκικο) — A slow or medium tempo dance with nine counts to the measure. See page 34.

The Tsiphte Teli

Song Index

Contributors

Markos Dragoumis (1934) studied Byzantine Music at Oxford. A professor of music history at the Athens Conservatory for over 30 years, he published in Greek and foreign journals on Byzantine music, Greek folk music and rebetika. He is supervisor of the Melpo Merlier Center for Greek Folk Music Studies.

Sakis Papadimitriou (1940) studied law. A radio producer for State Radio for over 30 years, he composed music for the theatre, published 22 books and contributed to numerous journals and anthologies of music and literature.

Ted Petrides (1928-1988) studied and researched widely Greek folk dance for 20 years. In addition to journal articles and notes for record album covers and inserts, he published two books on Greek folk dances.

Elias Petropoulos (1928-2003) studied law at the University of Thessaloniki, and Turkology in Paris, where he lived after 1975. A leading figure in folk tradition research, he was the first to record and document the Greek underworld. He published more than 80 books and almost 1,000 articles.

Elias Petropoulos, Ted Petrides (standing),
Sara Schneider, Sakis Papadimitriou,
Markos Dragoumis, Katharine Butterworth.
Photograph taken in 1975.